Model Writing for Ages 7–12

Are you looking for excellent writing models to support teaching writing, punctuation and grammar from the 2014 National Curriculum? *Model Writing for Ages 7–12* is a compilation of short, photocopiable texts including fiction, non-fiction and poetry that provides teachers with writing models for a wide range of genres, writing styles and topics while incorporating the National Curriculum obligations.

With stories ranging from historical accounts of the Vikings and the Blitz to a more sophisticated version of *Little Red Riding Hood*, and writing genres ranging from persuasive writing texts to newspaper reports, *Model Writing for Ages 7–12* provides teachers with an example for every eventuality. The perfect aid for teaching writing, each text is accompanied by a table listing which statutory assessment criteria it includes, as well as a blank table for pupils to collect examples themselves.

This invaluable text is essential for upper Key Stage 2 and lower Key Stage 3 teachers, particularly literacy coordinators and all those who lack confidence with the grammatical concepts in a text.

Leysa Henderson is a Specialist Leader in Education for Primary Literacy and Director of Kreative Futures Consulting and Training, UK.

Model Writing for Ages 7–12

Fiction, Non-Fiction and Poetry Texts Modelling Writing Expectations from the National Curriculum

Leysa Henderson

LONDON AND NEW YORK

First published 2018
by Routledge
2 Park Square, Milton Park, Abingdon, Oxon OX14 4RN

and by Routledge
711 Third Avenue, New York, NY 10017

Routledge is an imprint of the Taylor & Francis Group, an informa business

© 2018 Leysa Henderson

British Library Cataloguing in Publication Data
A catalogue record for this book is available from the British Library

Library of Congress Cataloging in Publication Data
Names: Henderson, Leysa, author.
Title: Model writing for ages 7–12 : fiction, non-fiction and poetry texts
modelling writing expectations from the national curriculum / Leysa Henderson.
Description: Abingdon, Oxon : New York, NY : Routledge, 2018.
Identifiers: LCCN 2017029016 | ISBN 9781138502536 (hardback) |
ISBN 9781138502581 (pbk.) | ISBN 9781315144962 (ebook)
Subjects: LCSH: Language arts (Elementary)–Great Britain. | Language arts
(Elementary)–Activity programs. | English language–Composition
and exercises–Study and teaching (Elementary)–Great Britain. |
Education and state–Great Britain.
Classification: LCC LB1576 .H3336 2018 | DDC 372.62/3–dc23
LC record available at https://lccn.loc.gov/2017029016

ISBN: 978-1-138-50253-6 (hbk)
ISBN: 978-1-138-50258-1 (pbk)
ISBN: 978-1-315-14496-2 (ebk)

Typeset in Helvetica and Comic Sans
by Out of House Publishing

Printed in the United Kingdom
by Henry Ling Limited

Contents

Acknowledgements   vii

Introduction   1

Part I: Fiction   5

1   The Cave   7
    Adventure and fantasy story

2   Death Is Everywhere   15
    Historical story about the plague

3   Description   23
    Adjective activity

4   Gold, Fire and Death   26
    Historical story about the Vikings landing at Lindisfarne

5   Red   34
    Fairy tale based on Little Red Riding Hood

6   The Blitz   45
    Historical story about the Blitz in a city during World War II

7   The Myth of Osiris and Isis   53
    Egyptian myth

Part II: Non-fiction   63

8   Biography of Louis Braille   65

9   Autobiography of Louis Braille   75

10 Vikings Plunder Unsuspecting Monastery   85
    Newspaper article on the landing of the Vikings at Lindisfarne

11 The Dunkirk Miracle   91
    Newspaper article on the rescue of the soldiers from the Dunkirk beaches in World War II

12 Letter Home from a Soldier   99
    Description of what is happening on the Dunkirk beaches

13 The Lifecycle of the Mayfly   107
    Information/explanation text

14 What Do You Cook a Fussy, Grumpy Dragon?   114
    Instructional text

15 Should Children Have Been Evacuated in World War II?   121
    Discussion

16 The Argument for Quitting Social Media   132
    Persuasive text

17 How Did the Ancient Egyptians Mummify Their Dead?   142
    Explanation text

Part III: Poetry   151

18 Using Poetry to Teach Grammar, Sentence Structure and Figurative Language   153

19 Angry Earth   156

20 The Island   158

21 If I Were…   160

22 I Wish…   162

23 Men of the Docks: Painting by George Bellows (1912)   164

24 Peace   166

25 A Winter's Morning: Poetry to Prose   168

26 Metaphor Poem   171

27 Personification Poem   173

Part IV: Grammar   175

28 Nouns and Noun Phrases   177

29 Pronouns   180

30 Determiners   183

31 Adjectives   184

32 Types of Adverbs   188

33 Subject–Verb Agreement   190

34 Conjunctions   192

35 Verbs   194

36 Inverted Commas   199

37 How to Use Colons and Semi-colons   200

38 Passive and Active Sentences   202

Acknowledgements

This book would not have been possible without the support of Darren Oakes. Also, a big thank you to Colin Playle who spent hours reviewing the book and, as a consequence, offering valuable advice.

Introduction

What is included in the book?

This book comprises photocopiable fiction, non-fiction and poetry texts, analysis and ideas as well as explanations on grammar conventions. The texts are purposefully written to exemplify the National Curriculum criteria and the end of Key Stage 2 interim assessment. However, there are times that the writer breaks with convention for writer's effect.

With the analysis, it would be impossible to include all the examples from the text in each criteria, so there is only a selection of examples. From this, the pupils will get an idea of what to look for and be able to identify further examples themselves.

Layout for the fiction and non-fiction texts

1 Example text
2 Blank table for the pupils to identify the criteria within the text
3 Teacher's notes and ideas
4 Teacher's version of the pupil's table with some examples from the text

In the poetry section, there are ideas and examples on how to use poetry to support word-class comprehension, vocabulary development, sentence construction and figurative language. There are explanations on the different types of figurative language appropriate to Key Stage 2 and early Key Stage 3. From each type of figurative language, you can develop the idea to deepen understanding. For example, you can look at different types of idioms and what they mean. This will be particularly useful for autistic pupils.

The book also contains a section on grammar. It includes areas that have not been included in the National Curriculum glossary or have not been clarified enough for teachers to have a clear understanding.

There are photocopiable tables which could be used for poetry or story writing to expand pupils' vocabulary use and word-class knowledge. These tables can also be used when rehearsing sentence structure.

HOW TO USE THE MODEL TEXTS

Before you meet the text

It is always more engaging if you introduce the topic with a launch lesson. This can consist of a video, story, drama production, museum visit, artefact, visitor or creating a crime scene for the pupils to solve. Once their interest has been ignited, the pupils will willingly follow you.

For example, with *The Cave*, you could create clues and leave objects around the classroom in the morning for the pupils to ascertain that a dragon had visited the classroom during the night and left things behind. With the Dunkirk news report, picture clues could be given to the pupils for them to work out what was happening on the Dunkirk beaches. This could then be supplemented with short video clips, audio speeches and mock-up newspaper reports.

Reading strategies

Good-quality reading leads to good-quality writing. The texts can be used in guided reading activities where the teacher can probe the pupils for greater meaning and structure of paragraphs as well as text structure. This, unfortunately, has been lost with the interim assessment sheet introduced in 2016.

Activities using the text could be used initially, such as unscrambling a cut-up version of the text. This will give you a chance to discuss structure and how one idea can lead on to another. It could also raise the point that some paragraphs or sections could feasibly occur in different parts of the texts while others would make the text sound clumsy or be incomprehensible.

Analyse as a reader (the effect on the reader) and then analyse as a writer (how the writer creates that effect). It is also important to read other quality examples of the same genre being covered as there is no one way to write something.

Content is always a struggle for teachers to cover; giving pupils enough to write about is an ever-occurring problem. Use the texts to collect ideas or information but also use other sources including videos, fiction and non-fiction books, photographs, paintings and interviews with pupils, teachers, parents or possibly visitors, to name a few suggestions. Some information can be made up even with historical or information texts. This is what happened with the dragon recipe. Most of the other texts are not completely accurate either, possibly with the exception of the mummification text, which is fairly precise according to scientific evidence.

Speaking and listening activities

Pupils need to rehearse sentence structure, identify text structure, collect and create imaginative ideas and possibly tap into the emotions of a character or event. This can all be done using speaking and listening activities.

Include drama conventions (see www.dramaresource.com/drama-strategies/), class, group or paired discussions, Pie Corbett style imitation and reading sentences out loud after construction. Use as many strategies as possible to get pupils to talk using the text type or talk about the actual content. This will reinforce the work done in guided reading.

Another activity would be to get pupils to put themselves into another person's shoes – perceptual positioning. An example is the dragon in *The Cave*. What would the dragon do after his precious stones had been stolen? How would he feel? What was the back story to the dragon? What would the aunt's story be in *Death is Everywhere*? Even with mummification, you could discuss the afterlife and what it means to different religions. These ideas could all lead to independent writing.

Vocabulary

Choose vocabulary you feel the pupils will not understand and do some pre-teaching before they read the text. This could involve getting them to match a picture or definition with a word.

Another activity could involve categorising the word class by identifying where the word is in the sentence. Word class is dependent on the position of the word in the sentence, although this is not always the case. However, adverbs are one of the few word classes that can move around the sentence and still remain an adverb. Pupils need to be mentally flexible to understand that many words can be categorised under several word classes and have different meanings.

Other lessons could focus on synonyms, antonyms, homographs, homophones or heteronyms.

Allow pupils to magpie words and phrases from the modelled text but be sure to remove it completely when they write, otherwise you will end up with 30 versions of the same thing.

Use the collected words and phrases to practise different sentence construction.

Structure

This is being lost in among the need to tick off grammatical elements required in the National Curriculum. Don't forget to keep a close rein on the need for clear paragraphs denoting just one point and clear text structure. This is fundamental for a text to make sense.

Start by getting pupils to identify the subject of each paragraph – sometimes you can challenge them to write it in under six words. Also, get pupils to bullet point the text structure. They need to have the big picture in their minds to be able to follow it.

Editing

Editing is underrated and underused and yet it should be a major element in the writing process. Published authors will have their work reviewed and edited several times before it comes to press so why is this not given the attention it deserves in a planned unit of work? For several reasons: teachers feel under pressure to get pupils to produce a long and tidy piece of writing in a very short time period; pupils don't like to edit or don't know how to edit; or teachers aren't precise with editing expectations.

This process should be demonstrated and flagged up at all stages of writing. During shared writing with the class, use this as a great opportunity to establish the importance of editing as you write. When pupils offer suggestions, press for more appropriate vocabulary choice, better constructed sentences, clearer paragraph organisation and pace, as well as constantly demonstrating re-reading the written passage to ensure it makes sense. This process might seem daunting or feel like it takes too long, but it is vital to show pupils how to construct and edit while they write.

If you have a class that is particularly reluctant to edit, ask them to craft their piece on the computer. They save the revised version as version 2, and make changes on the computer; they are more likely to improve their writing if it isn't handwritten. This can be repeated several times. They can then look back and compare their first and final version; it will show them how important it is to edit by the obvious vast improvement.

When writing a narrative, pupils can read it to a partner who acts it out at the same time. The partner must be strict with following the story instructions to show the writer any gaps or spurious time leaps which make the story confusing.

Another editing idea is to get the pupils to choose one picture for each paragraph. I did this with the Blitz story and pupils very quickly realised that their paragraphs were confusing and contained either too much or were too sparse.

Conclusion

Models are important but so are all the other stages of teaching how to write: teaching the content, genre criteria, reading and writing analysis, shared writing, sentence structure, vocabulary development, oral rehearsal, text structure, independent writing and editing. All these elements will lead to quality writing. But most of all, enjoy what you are teaching and be enthusiastic. If you don't, fake it till you make it.

PART I
Fiction

1   The Cave

Plot based on Pie Corbett's *Kassim and the Dragon*

Aiden never did like the mornings, especially when it was a school one, but he knew his mum had a bad habit of pulling him out of bed by his ear so he reluctantly dragged himself out of bed, got changed and hurtled downstairs. As he was rushing out of the house, his mum shouted, 'Remember, don't be lured into the Fearsome Dragon's lair!' As usual, Aiden totally ignored his mother's warning. Anyone who knew Aiden knew that he never did what he should do.

However, his confidence started to vanish as he came closer to the forest; it wasn't called the Forbidden Forest for nothing.

Arriving at its outskirts, Aiden, scared, edged his way cautiously in. Gnarled branches twisted like barbed wire barred his way and faces on the trunks of trees taunted him. Materialising through the branches, a blood-curdling howl pierced the melancholy silence. Around him, he could see shadows stalking like wolves waiting to ambush. Warily, gingerly, Aiden tiptoed deeper into the darkened depths of the forest, wondering why his journey to school always had to start with fear and trepidation. The forest had many secrets and he was a little afraid of finding them out but somehow he was propelled to discover them.

As he rounded the corner, looming out of the darkness, a granite boulder seemed to have appeared from nowhere. Aiden was sure it hadn't been there a minute ago, 'Maybe I've strayed from the path?' Aiden said out loud to reassure himself. He walked round the boulder and, on the other side, found that it was not a rock but the entrance to a dark, damp cave. Water could be heard dripping from the ceiling and a faint bubbling sound echoed through the tunnels – was it a stream, wondered Aiden. The entrance stretched its mouth wide open, inviting all explorers to enter at their peril.

Aiden, who was always curious, made a decision that he was going to be late for school and explore the cave instead. After taking a few steps in, he stopped and allowed his eyes to adjust to the darkness. While standing there, he remembered he had a wind-up torch in his school bag. 'I knew this would come in handy sometime,' Aiden said a little too loudly.

Going deeper into the cave, Aiden came to a crossroads; he decided it didn't matter which way he went, so he turned left. Unfortunately, he didn't notice the sign carved on the wall saying Dragon's Canyon.

The ground started to slope downwards, at first gently and then much steeper. As it became steeper, it became harder to hold the torch and negotiate the rocks but Aiden was determined not to give up. Ahead of him, he spied a faint beam shining directly from the roof on to something that seemed to glisten. Slowly but surely, he approached the object that was shimmering. Confused, he walked round it unable to understand what he was seeing. He couldn't believe that this had never been found before. Aiden had never seen anything like it before.

Reaching out to pick it up, he held it up to the light, amazed at the rainbows dancing off it. He had never seen such a large diamond in all his life. In his excitement, he grabbed another one and another one but just as he was about to help himself to another one, he heard a spine-chilling, ear-piercing cry that made his hair stand on end and his heart stop beating. He knew, instinctively, that trouble was near.

The cry was a cry of anger, of torment, of greed. The creature had seen Aiden take the jewels, he was stealing what rightly belonged to him. No one had a right to steal his diamonds; no one was going to deprive the Fearsome Dragon of his possessions. He was going to teach this little upstart a lesson.

At first, the dragon's movement was awkward because he had moved very little over the last decade, but soon his limbs started to work again. Rearing up on his hind legs, the Fearsome Dragon breathed fire from the pit of his belly and aimed at Aiden. The flames shot across the cave and licked at Aiden's coat-tails – singeing them. Aiden didn't hang around to wait for more; he turned, still clutching the diamonds, and ran in what he thought, or rather hoped, was the direction he had come from.

Petrified but focused, Aiden practically leapt up the steep slope leaving behind him an avalanche of rocks. With very little effort, he made it to the crossroads. Quickly calculating his direction, he turned right and hoped that the tunnel mouth was only just round the corner.

Daylight lay ahead of him; he was relieved to see the exit and rushed out to breathe the fresh air of freedom.

Momentarily, Aiden strained to hear if he was being followed but not a sound was heard. Not taking any chances, he decided to run home and hide. Not so brave now!

With fear in his heart and wings for feet, Aiden made it home quicker than he had ever done before. Crashing through the door, racing upstairs two by two stairs at a time and finally hurling himself into his room, Aiden was immensely relieved to be safe.

It was then that he remembered the diamonds but when he opened his hand to admire his new-found wealth they were no longer there. In place of the glistening jewels was a pile of dust; the whole adventure had come to nothing.

For the rest of his life, Aiden never forgot the exciting adventure yet also never wanted to repeat it.

Analyse the text

Table 1.1

Criteria	Examples from the text	
Describe setting and character to create atmosphere		
Cohesive devices within and across sentences and paragraphs (including adverbials, determiners, conjunctions, pronouns and ellipses)		
Different verb forms		
Wide range of clauses in varying position Subordinate clauses		
Co-ordinating and subordinating conjunctions	Co-ordinating	Subordinating
Exclamation marks		
Commas for lists (objects and actions)		
Apostrophes for contraction		

(continued)

Table 1.1 (*cont.*)

	Adverbs	Preposition phrases	Expanded noun phrases
Apostrophes for possession			
Creating atmosphere and integrating dialogue to convey character and advance the action			
Passive sentences			
Modal verbs			
Use of adverbs, preposition phrases and expanded noun phrases to add detail			
Inverted commas			
Commas for clarity			
Punctuation for parenthesis			
Semi-colons to mark the boundary between independent clauses			
Hyphens			

Teacher's notes and ideas

1 Pupils summarise the story in 300 words, then in 150 words and down to 50 words.

2 Get the pupils to write down the order of the story (see below). They can then plan their own story using the same structure but adding their own detail.

3 Take each section of the story and teach a new element, either vocabulary, sentence structure or figurative language between each section. The pupils can edit the story as they go along. So, for example you could teach personification to describe the journey through the Forbidden Forest; pupils could then go back and see where they could potentially add personification earlier on. Also, later on in their story, they should attempt to include personification.

4 During the editing process, pupils read their story to a partner and the partner acts it out, ensuring that they follow the exact instructions and do not fill in the gaps. This helps the writer to identify areas that they could improve.

5 Write a story from the dragon's perspective. It could include its back story as to how it came to live in the cave. It could also feature how the dragon acquired the diamonds and why he was protecting them. Pupils could extend the story to show what happens to the dragon after the diamonds were stolen. For example, maybe he died because the diamonds were his elixir for eternal life and once gone it made him mortal.

6 This story is an extended and embellished version of *Kassim and the Dragon*, written by Pie Corbett. You could use this as a start point for the imitation stage and then use this story to highlight the invention stage.

Structure of the story

1 Aiden reluctantly gets ready for school
2 Mum warns him of danger
3 Walks to the edge of the Forbidden Forest
4 Description of the Forbidden Forest as he walks through it
5 Finds a cave entrance
6 The journey through the cave
7 Finds the diamonds
8 The dragon catches him stealing the diamonds
9 The dragon chases him out of the cave
10 Arrives home and finds that the diamonds are now dust

Table 1.2

Criteria	Examples from the text
Describe setting and character to create atmosphere	Arriving at its outskirts, Aiden, scared, edged his way cautiously in. Gnarled branches twisted like barbed wire barred his way and faces on the trunks of trees taunted him. Materialising through the branches, a blood-curdling howl pierced the melancholy silence. Around him, he could see shadows stalking like wolves waiting to ambush. Warily, gingerly, Aiden tiptoed deeper into the black depths of the forest, wondering why his journey to school always had to start with fear and trepidation. The forest had many secrets and he was a little afraid of finding them out but somehow he was propelled to discover them. As he rounded the corner, looming out of the darkness, a granite boulder seemed to have appeared from nowhere.

(continued)

Table 1.2 (*cont.*)

	At first, the dragon's movement was awkward because he had moved very little over the last decade, but soon his limbs started to work again. Rearing up on his hind legs, the Fearsome Dragon breathed fire from the pit of his belly and aimed at Aiden. The flames shot across the cave and licked at his coat-tails – singeing them.
Cohesive devices within and across sentences and paragraphs (including adverbials, determiners, conjunctions, pronouns and ellipses)	Aiden never did like the mornings, especially when it was a school one (The 'one' refers to the morning.) …but he knew his mum had a bad habit of pulling him out of bed by his ear. (Refers back to the name Aiden in the first sentence.) However, his confidence started to vanish… (Refers back to the inference that he was confident because he ignores warnings and does what he wants to do.) He couldn't believe that this had never been found <u>before</u>. Aiden was sure <u>it</u> hadn't been there a minute ago. (Refers to the boulder.)
Different verb forms	knew was rushing out remember, don't be lured never did what he should do. wasn't called arriving could see seemed to have appeared hadn't been have strayed was going to be knew this would come was seeing couldn't believe had never seen reaching out could find and held it up had never seen
Wide range of clauses in varying position Subordinate clauses	As he was rushing out of the house, his mum shouted, 'Remember, don't be lured into the Fearsome Dragon's lair!' While standing there, he remembered he had a wind-up torch in his school bag. Aiden, who was always curious, made a decision that he was going to be late for school and explore the cave instead. At first, the dragon's movement was awkward because he had moved very little over the last decade, but soon his limbs started to work again.

Co-ordinating and subordinating conjunctions	Co-ordinating	Subordinating
	and but so for yet	as while after because when

Exclamation marks	'Remember, don't be lured into the Fearsome Dragon's lair!' Not so brave now!
Commas for lists (objects and actions)	…he reluctantly dragged himself out of bed, got changed and hurtled downstairs. Crashing through the door, racing upstairs two by two stairs at a time and finally hurling himself into his room, Aiden was immensely relieved to be safe.
Apostrophes for contraction	don't wasn't hadn't didn't couldn't

Apostrophes for possession	dragon's		mother's
Creating atmos- phere and integrating dia- logue to convey character and advance the action	'Remember, don't be lured into the Fearsome Dragon's lair!' 'Maybe I have strayed from the path,' Aiden said out loud to reassure himself. 'I knew this would come in handy sometime,' Aiden said a little too loudly.		
Passive sentences	...it wasn't called the Forbidden Forest for nothing. ...he was being followed... ...this had never been found before.		
Modal verbs	should, could, would		
Use of adverbs, preposition phrases and expanded noun phrases to add detail	**Adverbs**	**Preposition phrases**	**Expanded noun phrases**
	especially reluctantly totally cautiously warily gingerly only loudly unfortunately gently surely directly instinctively practically quickly momentarily immensely with fear and trepidation with very little effort	on the other side on the wall saying Dragon's Canyon at its outskirts at the rainbows dancing off it as he rounded the corner out of the house into the Fearsome Dragon's lair	a bad habit of pulling him out of bed by his ear the fresh air of freedom a cry of anger, of tor- ment, of greed the pile of shimmering gems a right to steal his diamonds the Fearsome Dragon of his possessions a large diamond in all his life
Inverted commas	'Remember, don't be lured into the Fearsome Dragon's lair!' 'Maybe I have strayed from the path,' Aiden said out loud to reassure himself. 'I knew this would come in handy sometime,' Aiden said a little too loudly.		
Commas for clarity	As he was rushing out of the house, his mum shouted, 'Remember, don't be lured into the Fearsome Dragon's lair!' At first, the dragon's movement was awkward because he had moved very little over the last decade, but soon his limbs started to work again. For the rest of his life, Aiden never forgot the exciting adventure yet also never wanted to repeat it. Crashing through the door, racing up stairs two by two stairs at a time and finally hurling himself into his room, Aiden was immensely relieved to be safe.		

(continued)

Table 1.2 (*cont.*)

Punctuation for parenthesis	The flames shot across the cave and licked at his coat-tails – singeing them.
Semi-colons to mark the boundary between independent clauses	However, his confidence started to vanish as he came closer to the forest; it wasn't called the Forbidden Forest for nothing. No one had a right to steal his diamonds; no one was going to deprive the Fearsome Dragon of his possessions. Aiden didn't hang around to wait for more; he turned, still clutching the diamonds… Daylight lay ahead of him; he was relieved to see the exit and rushed out to breathe the fresh air of freedom. In place of the glistening jewels was a pile of dust; the whole adventure had come to nothing.
Hyphens	blood-curdling ear-piercing spine-chilling

2   Death Is Everywhere

This story doesn't have a happy ending but it does have an ending. It won't make you laugh uncontrollably but it will help you to understand how difficult life was for many people hundreds of years ago.

It was 1665 and Charles II was on the throne. He was an unpopular king, especially with the poor, as he did not rule wisely and justly. During his reign, there were two major catastrophes from which neither the rich nor poor could escape. One was the Great Fire of London, the other... Well, this story will recount the other.

This tragic tale starts in a tiny village called Eyam in Derbyshire. Yes, it's a real village. More importantly, it was a courageous village.

Running through the woods in Eyam, Tom – our principal character – weaved his way between the low hung branches. Indignation coursed through his blood.

'It wasn't fair,' he thought, 'I'm always the one that gets shouted at.'

Tom decided there and then that it was time to leave home, time to travel to London to make his own way in life. He said no goodbyes and told no one where he was going. He didn't think about the consequences of his silent disappearance. This is something he will think about later and something he may well regret, afterwards.

The journey to London was arduous and long so it won't be told here. What I can tell you is that when he did arrive, he was hungry and very lonely.

Looking up at the West Gate entrance, Tom wondered, not for the first time, how he was going to find his aunt and uncle in among the labyrinth of streets. As he walked into the hustle and bustle of the narrow, cobbled London alleyways, it was as if – compared with Eyam – he had stepped from a world of silence into a world of chaos.

Street vendors shouted, advertising their wares; dunghills were piled up against wooden houses releasing their venomous odour, and rotting rubbish floated along the sour rivers that interlaced the cobbled streets and crooked houses. Tom was shocked and saddened by these scenes, scenes which offended his sense of order and cleanliness.

'I suppose I will have to get used to this,' Tom muttered to himself with resignation.

There was one particularly hideous cry rising above the clamour from the many street vendors, which sent a paralysing chill down Tom's spine.

'BRING OUT YOUR DEAD! BRING OUT YOUR DEAD!'

He followed the cry and was astounded to see a pile of dead bodies, actual corpses, stacked up high on a cart. This didn't seem right: in fact, it was all wrong! Why were there so many dead bodies? What were people dying from?

The streets were getting darker and darker and Tom knew that he must find his aunt and uncle's house soon; with no street lighting, it was the time for the robbers, drunks and kidnappers to take to the dark corners.

At last, he reached his uncle's house. Tom knocked tentatively; the door swung open and there stood a dishevelled woman.

'Tom!' she exclaimed, 'How lovely to see you! Come in, come in.'

His uncle, however, wasn't quite so pleased to see him; stone-faced, he just grunted and sat down by the fire. Then, after a while the uncle looked up and said, 'You had better come to work with me tomorrow. If you are going to live with us, we need the money to support another mouth to feed.'

Tom woke early, excited about earning some money but he hadn't realised that working for a tanners was going to be a hard, dirty and particularly smelly job.

On their way home, his uncle spoke about the Black Death, which was rampaging through London. They passed many houses with a red cross on the door.

'Why the red cross, uncle?' Tom enquired.

'These are very sad times, Tom. Many thousands of people are dying from an invisible enemy. Once a red cross has been put on your front door, everyone inside is destined to die because someone has fallen ill with the Black Death and no other member of the household is allowed either to leave or enter. The only way they leave is in a bag – dead.'

His uncle fell silent for a while. Eventually, he went on to explain the Black Death symptoms. 'The skin turns black, you get a splitting headache, a fever takes hold, there are swellings under the arms, the tongue swells up so the victim can't breathe and finally you start to vomit violently. It only takes a couple of days for a person to die.'

When Tom woke up the next morning, he was surprised to see that only his aunt was downstairs.

'Where is my uncle?'

Tom's aunt looked down and mumbled, 'He has a splitting headache. I think he will stay at home today. Tomorrow he'll be better.'

Tom wasn't reassured at all; he worried all day so when the bell rang signalling the end of the day, he raced home.

Tom stopped abruptly, wide-eyed, in front of his aunt and uncle's door. There on the front door painted large and clear was a red cross.

This was not the end of Tom's tragic tale but it is the end of this story. The rest is for another day and for another story.

Analyse the text

Table 2.1

Criteria	Examples from the text	
Describe setting and character to create atmosphere		
Cohesive devices within and across sentences and paragraphs (including adverbials, determiners, conjunctions, pronouns and ellipses)		
Different verb forms for meaning and effect		
Co-ordinating and subordinating conjunctions	Co-ordinating	Subordinating
Question marks		
Exclamation marks		
Commas for lists		
Apostrophes for contraction		

(continued)

Table 2.1 (*cont.*)

Apostrophes for possession			
Integrating dialogue (inverted commas)			
Passive sentences			
Modal verbs			
Wide range of clause structures in varying position (commas for clarity) Subordinate clauses			
Use of adverbs, preposition phrases and expanded noun phrases to add detail	Adverbs	Preposition phrases	Expanded noun phrases
Hyphens			
Semi-colons to mark the boundary between independent clauses			
Managing shifts of formality			

Teacher's notes and ideas

This story is based on facts gleaned from history. The reason Eyam was chosen was because the story could be continued with Tom returning home to find his village had been sealed off. The villagers decided to do this after a travelling salesman brought the plague with him to Derbyshire. The pupils could study the history and courage of the people of Eyam.

This links with Berlie Doherty's story, the *Children of Winter* (www.berliedoherty.com/novels/children-of-winter.html).

The pupils could write a story from two perspectives: the hardships of somebody from the village and Tom returning home. The two stories could be woven together. Or a diary could be written, a newspaper article or a letter from a villager to a friend or family outside the village.

Structure of the story

1 Introducing the plague
2 Tom leaving home
3 Arriving in London
4 Sights and sounds of London
5 Arriving at the uncle's house
6. Going to work at the tanners
7 Uncle falls ill
8 Goes to work on his own
9 Arrives home to find a red cross on the door
10 Conclusion that links with the introduction (potentially leads the story back home for Tom to discover that the plague had reached his home village – Eyam)

Table 2.2

Criteria	Examples from the text
Describe setting and character to create atmosphere	Looking up at the West Gate entrance, Tom wondered, not for the first time, how he was going to find his aunt and uncle in among the labyrinth of streets. As he walked into the hustle and bustle of the narrow, cobbled London alleyways, it was as if – compared with Eyam – he had stepped from a world of silence into a world of chaos.
Street vendors shouted, advertising their wares; dunghills were piled up against wooden houses releasing their venomous odour and rotting rubbish floated along the sour rivers that interlaced the cobbled streets and crooked houses. Tom was shocked and saddened by these scenes, scenes which offended his sense of order and cleanliness.
The streets were getting darker and darker and Tom knew that he must find his aunt and uncle's house soon; with no street lighting, it was the time for the robbers, drunks and kidnappers to take to the dark corners.

(*continued*)

Table 2.2 (*cont.*)

	His uncle, however, wasn't quite so pleased to see him; stone-faced, he just grunted and sat down by the fire. Then, after a while the uncle looked up and said, 'You had better come to work with me tomorrow. If you are going to live with us, we need the money to support another mouth to feed.'
	'These are very sad times, Tom. Many thousands of people are dying from an invisible enemy. Once a red cross has been put on your front door, everyone inside is destined to die because someone has fallen ill with the Black Death and no other member of the household is allowed either to leave or enter. The only way they leave is in a bag – dead.'
	His uncle fell silent for a while. Eventually, he went on to explain the Black Death symptoms. 'The skin turns black, you get a splitting headache, a fever takes hold, there are swellings under the arms, the tongue swells up so the victim can't breathe and finally you start to vomit violently. It only takes a couple of days for a person to die.'
Cohesive devices within and across sentences and paragraphs (including adverbials, determiners, conjunctions, pronouns and ellipses)	<u>During</u> his reign… <u>This</u> was not the end of Tom's tragic tale but <u>it</u> is the end of this story. The rest is for another day and for another story. Tom decided there and then <u>that it</u> was time to leave home, time to travel to London to make <u>his own way</u> in life. <u>These</u> are very sad times, Tom. '<u>I'm</u> always the <u>one</u> that gets shouted at.' One was the Great Fire of London, <u>the other</u>… <u>After a while</u>… <u>At last</u>, he reached his uncle's house.

Different verb forms for meaning and effect	does	to find
	will help	had stepped
	could	BRING OUT
	called	are going to live
	running	was rampaging
	was going	has been put
	will think	is allowed

Co-ordinating and subordinating conjunctions	Co-ordinating	Subordinating
	and	which
	but	as
	so	as if
		when
		if
		after a while
		then
		once

Question marks	Why were there so many dead bodies? What were people dying from? 'Why the red cross, uncle?' 'Where is my uncle?'
Exclamation marks	'Tom!' 'How lovely to see you!...' 'BRING OUT YOUR DEAD! BRING OUT YOUR DEAD!' This didn't seem right: in fact, it was all wrong!
Commas for lists	...it was the time for the robbers, drunks and kidnappers to take to the dark corners. The skin turns black, you get a splitting headache, a fever takes hold, there are swellings under the arms, the tongue swells up so the victim can't breathe and finally you start to vomit violently.
Apostrophes for contraction	doesn't　　　　　　　　didn't won't　　　　　　　　　wasn't it's　　　　　　　　　　hadn't I'm　　　　　　　　　　can't wasn't　　　　　　　　　he'll
Apostrophes for possession	uncle's house　　　　　　Tom's aunt
Integrating dialogue (inverted commas)	'It wasn't fair,' he thought, 'I'm always the one that gets shouted at.' 'I suppose I will have to get used to this,' Tom muttered 'BRING OUT YOUR DEAD! BRING OUT YOUR DEAD!' 'Tom!' she exclaimed, 'How lovely to see you! Come in, come in.' 'You had better come to work with me tomorrow. If you are going to live with us, we need the money to support another mouth to feed.' 'These are very sad times, Tom. Many thousands of people are dying from an invisible enemy. Once a red cross has been put on your front door, everyone inside is destined to die because someone has fallen ill with the Black Death and no other member of the household is allowed either to leave or enter. The only way they leave is in a bag – dead.'
Passive sentences	Tom was shocked and saddened by these scenes...
Modal verbs	can, will, must, could
Wide range of clause structures in varying position (commas for clarity) Subordinate clauses	He was an unpopular king, especially with the poor, as he did not rule wisely and justly. As he walked into the hustle and bustle of the narrow, cobbled London alleyways, it was as if – compared with Eyam – he had stepped from a world of silence into a world of chaos. Once a red cross has been put on your front door, everyone inside is destined to die because someone has fallen ill with the Black Death and no other member of the household is allowed either to leave or enter. Tom wasn't reassured at all; he worried all day so when the bell rang signalling the end of the day, he raced home. Looking up at the West Gate entrance, Tom wondered, not for the first time, how he was going to find his aunt and uncle in among the labyrinth of streets.

(continued)

Table 2.2 (*cont.*)

Use of adverbs, preposition phrases and expanded noun phrases to add detail	Adverbs	Preposition phrases	Expanded noun phrases
	uncontrollably wisely justly especially importantly lonely particularly tentatively particularly smelly early only eventually finally violently abruptly	from an invisible enemy into the hustle and bustle of the narrow, cobbled London alleyways in front of his aunt and uncle's door at the West Gate entrance from a world of silence into a world of chaos	rotting rubbish floated the sour rivers that interlaced the cobbled streets and crooked houses the hustle and bustle of the narrow, cobbled London alleyways dunghills were piled up against wooden houses releasing their venomous odour a world of silence into a world of chaos
Hyphens	stone-faced		wide-eyed
Semi-colons to mark the boundary between independent clauses	Street vendors shouted, advertising their wares; dunghills were piled up against wooden houses releasing their venomous odour and rotting rubbish floated along the sour rivers that interlaced the cobbled streets and crooked houses. The streets were getting darker and darker and Tom knew that he must find his aunt and uncle's house soon; with no street lighting, it was the time for the robbers, drunks and kidnappers to take to the dark corners. His uncle, however, wasn't quite so pleased to see him; stone-faced, he just grunted and sat down by the fire. Tom knocked tentatively; the door swung open and there stood a dishevelled woman. Tom wasn't reassured at all; he worried all day so when the bell rang signalling the end of the day, he raced home.		
Managing shifts of formality	This is shown by the story being punctuated by a narrator, which uses a behind-the-scenes perspective. In the introduction, the text uses a historical report format: 'It was 1665 and Charles II was on the throne. He was an unpopular king, especially with the poor, as he did not rule wisely and justly. During his reign, there were two major catastrophes from which neither the rich nor poor could escape. One was the Great Fire of London, the other… Well, this story will recount the other.' It then moves on to the retelling of a story by accessing the characters' feelings: 'It wasn't fair,' he thought, 'I'm always the one that gets shouted at.' This is more informal. This is followed by the retelling of his story. The story finally ends with the narrator hinting that there is more to the story.		

3   Description

Read the following passage and underline all of the adjectives

In front of the towering temple, the creature lay slumped motionless on the crumbling steps. Its blazing red eyes stared helplessly out at the villagers. Stillness lay all around. Even the wind had nothing to say.

As the evening sun streamed down through the dust, the creature's fluorescent green slime glistened on its scaly leather skin. Sharpened claws protruded threateningly from short but powerful arms. Its mouth curled its way round the deadly fangs. Despite its grotesque appearance, I felt sorry for it. In place of a lethal beast lay a creature breathing its last breath. A creature which has never known kindness.

Which passage do you think describes the monster without slowing the story down? Give your reasons.

1 As the evening sun streamed down through the dust, the monster's fluorescent green slime glistened on its scaly leather skin. Sharpened claws protruded threateningly from short but powerful arms. Its mouth curled its way round deadly fangs. Despite its grotesque appearance, I felt sorry for it. In place of a lethal beast lay a creature breathing its last breath. A creature which has never known kindness.

2 *As the sun streamed down through the dust, the monster's slime glistened on its skin. Its claws protruded threateningly from its arms. Its mouth curled its way round fangs. Despite its appearance, I felt sorry for it. In place of a beast lay a creature breathing its last breath. A creature which has never known kindness.*

3 As the hot golden evening sun streamed down through the light grey dust, the monster's fluorescent green slime glistened on its scaly leather skin. Sharpened dangerous claws protruded threateningly from short, hairy but powerful arms. Its thin, crooked mouth curled its way round deadly, yellow fangs. Despite its grotesque and unusual appearance, I felt sorry for it. In place of a lethal, ferocious beast lay a vulnerable creature breathing its last breath. A friendless creature which has never known kindness.

Find all the adjectives in each paragraph.

Table 3.1

Paragraph	Adjectives
1	
2	
3	
Add your own adjectives	

Add some more adjectives of your own to describe a monster and write your own passage. Be careful that you use good adjectives and not too many.

Teacher's notes and ideas

This is an exercise on the correct use of adjectives; pupils either use too many or ones that add no value to the story.

When they write their own description, give the pupils a list of adjectives to choose from and then a thesaurus for them to find their own. It would help if they have a picture of some monsters to describe.

Some adjectives have an '–ed' suffix and some '–ing'; this can confuse pupils as they see them as a verb. This is when it is really important to teach noun phrases, particularly the pre-modifying element: Determiner + adjective + noun.

Answers

In front of the <u>towering</u> temple, the creature lay slumped <u>motionless</u> on the <u>crumbling</u> steps. Its <u>blazing red</u> eyes stared helplessly out at the villagers. Stillness lay all around. Even the wind had nothing to say.

As the <u>evening</u> sun streamed down through the dust, the creature's <u>fluorescent</u> <u>green</u> slime glistened on its <u>scaly</u> <u>leather</u> skin. <u>Sharpened</u> claws protruded threateningly from <u>short</u> but <u>powerful</u> arms. Its mouth curled its way round <u>deadly</u> fangs. Despite its <u>grotesque</u> appearance, I felt sorry for it. In place of a <u>lethal</u> beast lay a creature breathing its <u>last</u> breath. A creature which has never known kindness.

Table 3.2

Paragraph	Adjectives	
1	evening	scaly
	fluorescent	leather
	green	short
	sharpened	powerful
	deadly	lethal
	grotesque	last
2	slime	last
3	hot	powerful
	golden	thin
	evening	crooked
	light	deadly
	grey	yellow
	fluorescent	grotesque
	green	unusual
	scaly	lethal
	leather	ferocious
	sharpened	vulnerable
	dangerous	last
	short	friendless
	hairy	

4 Gold, Fire and Death

It was the year 793 and England was enjoying a peace that, unknown to the English, was not going to last for long. In a small place in the north-east of England, the world was about to be turned upside down. This year marked the start of many hostile raids, hundreds of deaths and much misery: this was the beginning of the period of savage Viking history.

Alfred was an orphan; he had lost his parents to a fever two years earlier. He was, however, one of the lucky ones, as the St Cuthbert's Monks of Lindisfarne had invited him to live with them – as long as he helped in the kitchen; and, because of their kindness, Alfred had a sense of loyalty to these old and industrious religious people. He felt safe at Lindisfarne; it was a place where peace lived, good people prospered and happiness danced among the trees.

However, the peace of the monastery was soon to be violently shattered.

Early one misty summer morning, Alfred was asked to collect the vegetables from the garden for the lunchtime stew. Normally, he was not a naughty boy, but he loved the water's edge first thing in the morning, and today it was so tempting to stand and watch the sun rise above the horizon and enjoy the way it twinkled and shimmered on the sea's still surface.

As he stood looking out over the horizon, he noticed what appeared to be red and white sails blowing in the wind, floating delicately over the water; it was, he thought, an enchanting sight, but how wrong could he be? What he didn't realise was that this was not just beauty; it was danger, and the arrival of these longboats would change his life forever, and certainly not for the better!

As the ships drew closer, Alfred noticed the glint of swords and axes in the hands of the warriors aboard them. He decided that the shore was not a safe place to be, so he rapidly hid behind a sand dune to watch the longboats as they moved quickly forward and slid effortlessly onto the shore, as if they were skating.

'Who are they? Where had they come from?' thought Alfred. Then, listening and watching intently, Alfred heard the men shout out as they landed.

'Kill anyone you see and burn all the buildings!' ordered the lead warrior.

'Yes, Sweyn Forkbeard!' the men chorused.

Sweyn Forkbeard continued to yell, 'Take what you want as your prize: gold, silver and food – anything!'

The men rushed from the boats towards the monastery, roaring to intimidate the monks.

Alfred was terrified. His blood froze and so did he. He knew that the monks were defenceless against these fearsome warriors.

Suddenly, he sprang into action and followed the savage men, being careful not to be seen. He watched in horror as the monks ran for their lives and the raiders plunged their swords deep into the innocent victims, throwing their axes at the heads of the fleeing monks and stabbing anyone they could catch. The cold-blooded raiders killed everyone who lived at the monastery. Only Alfred, who had remained hidden, stayed alive to witness the terrifying event.

He watched them take all the gold and religious treasures, drag the sheep towards the boats and finally set light to the monastery itself: Norsemen, without conscience, without guilt, without faith.

'So much gold and so easy to take it and not one of my men has been killed! Those monks are slow-witted and useless,' thundered Sweyn Forkbeard. He laughed and laughed until he ran out of laughter.

When the raiders finally left, Alfred looked at the devastation. All the monks had been killed, the treasure plundered and the monastery was no more.

'Where should I go now? What am I going to do? My home has been destroyed, my life has been ripped apart.'

Alfred sat down and watched the smouldering remains of the monastery: his home, and now, his past life. The glorious early morning of sunshine and beauty and happiness had been transformed by slaughter into a black, horrible and fearful day of terror. The year 793: and a day never to be forgotten. Alfred sighed, stood up, took the deepest of breaths, squared his shoulders and then stepped slowly away from the shore to make his own history...

Analyse the text

Table 4.1

Criteria	Examples from the text	
Describe setting and character to create atmosphere		
Cohesive devices within and across sentences and paragraphs (including adverbials, determiners, pronouns, ellipses and conjunctions)		
Different verb forms		
Co-ordinating and subordinating conjunctions	**Co-ordinating**	**Subordinating**
Question marks		
Exclamation marks		
Commas for lists/actions		
Apostrophes for contraction		
Apostrophes for possession		
Create atmosphere and integrating dialogue (inverted commas)		

Modal verbs			
Passive sentences			
Wide range of clause structures in varying position Subordinate clauses			
Use of adverbs, preposition phrases and expanded noun phrases to add detail	Adverbs	Preposition phrases	Expanded noun phrases
Commas for clarity			
Punctuation for parenthesis			
Semi-colons to mark the boundary between independent clauses			
Colons			
Hyphens			

Teacher's notes and ideas

This story can be used prior to the newspaper article on the Lindisfarne raid by the Vikings. If you can learn it verbatim, then you can retell the story; this makes it more engaging for your class. Alternatively, you could use this as a story in its own right.

If you are courageous enough, dress up as a Viking (Sweyn Forkbeard) and the pupils can ask you questions about the raid. Or, after some research, the pupils become the experts.

This is a good opportunity to do a freeze-frame activity. Maybe avoid the complete re-enactment of death and destruction unless you are very confident with your class.

Structure of the story

1   Introduction to the time and place
2   Brief explanation of why Alfred is living with the monks
3   Alfred sent to pick the vegetables and goes to the water's edge
4   Alfred sees the Vikings arrive
5   Description of the Vikings/boats
6   Vikings give orders
7   Men rush up to the monastery
8   Alfred follows to witness the event
9   The Vikings kill all the monks
10   They loot the monastery for treasures and food
11   The devastation which is left behind
12   The uncertainty of Alfred's future

Table 4.2

Criteria	Examples from the text
Describe setting and character to create atmosphere	However, the peace of the monastery was soon to be violently shattered. Early one misty summer morning, Alfred was asked to collect the vegetables from the garden for the lunchtime stew. Normally, he was not a naughty boy, but he loved the water's edge first thing in the morning, and today it was so tempting to stand and watch the sun rise above the horizon and enjoy the way it twinkled and shimmered on the sea's still surface. As he stood looking out over the horizon, he noticed what appeared to be red and white sails blowing in the wind, floating delicately over the water; it was, he thought, an enchanting sight, but how wrong could he be? What he didn't realise was that this was not just beauty; it was danger, and the arrival of these longboats would change his life forever, and certainly not for the better!
Cohesive devices within and across sentences and paragraphs (including adverbials, determiners, conjunctions, pronouns and ellipses)	<u>However</u>, the peace of the monastery was soon to be violently shattered. (Refers back to the previous paragraph.) As he stood looking out over the horizon, he noticed what appeared to be red and white sails blowing in the wind, floating delicately over the water; it was, he thought, an enchanting sight, but how wrong could he be? What he didn't realise was <u>that this</u> was not just beauty, it was danger, and the arrival of these longboats would change his life for-ever, and certainly not for the better! (Refers back to the arrival of the ships and the inference of their impact on his future life.) Alfred was terrified. His blood froze and so did he. He knew that the monks were defenceless against these fearsome warriors. (Refers back to the previous paragraph and the mention of 'men'.)

	'Those monks are slow-witted and useless,' thundered Sweyn Forkbeard. (Determiner – demonstrative.) Only Alfred, who had remained hidden, stayed alive to witness the terrifying event. ('Only' – adverb stating that he was the only one left alive as the monks had been murdered. 'Who' – relates to Alfred and 'the terrifying event' – refers to the whole story.)	
Different verb forms	had lost invited was asked to watch could are would (to denote future tense)	listening and watching kill had remained have been killed had been killed should has been ripped
Co-ordinating and subordinating conjunctions	**Co-ordinating** and but so	**Subordinating** because when as until as long as
Question marks	…how wrong could he be? Who are they? Where had they come from? 'Where should I go now? What am I going to do?...'	
Exclamation marks	What he didn't realise was that this was not just beauty; it was danger, and the arrival of these longboats would change his life forever, and certainly not for the better! 'Kill anyone you see and burn all the buildings!' ordered the lead warrior. 'Yes, Sweyn Forkbeard!' the men chorused. 'Take what you want as your prize: gold, silver and food – anything!' 'So much gold and so easy to take it and not one of my men has been killed!'	
Commas for lists	Gold, Fire and Death He watched them take all the gold and religious treasures, drag the sheep towards the boats and finally set light to the monastery itself: Norsemen, without conscience, without guilt, without faith. …many hostile raids, hundreds of deaths and much misery…	
Apostrophes for contraction	didn't	
Apostrophes for possession	St Cuthbert's Monks of Lindisfarne water's edge sea's still surface	
Create atmosphere and integrating dialogue (inverted commas)	As the ships drew closer, Alfred noticed the glint of swords and axes in the hands of the warriors aboard them. He decided that the shore was not a safe place to be, so he rapidly hid behind a sand dune to watch the longboats as they moved quickly forward and slid effortlessly onto the shore, as if they were skating.	

(*continued*)

Table 4.2 (*cont.*)

	'Who are they? Where had they come from?' whispered Alfred. Then, listening and watching intently, Alfred heard the men shout out as they landed. 'Kill anyone you see and burn all the buildings!' ordered the lead warrior. 'Yes, Sweyn Forkbeard!' the men chorused. Sweyn Forkbeard continued to yell, 'Take what you want as your prize: gold, silver and food – anything!' The men rushed from the boats towards the monastery, roaring to intimidate the monks. Alfred was terrified. His blood froze and so did he. He knew that the monks were defenceless against these fearsome warriors. 'So much gold and so easy to take it and not one of my men has been killed! Those monks are slow-witted and useless,' thundered Sweyn Forkbeard. 'Where should I go now? What am I going to do? My home has been destroyed, my life has been ripped apart.'
Modal verbs	could, should, would
Passive sentences	Alfred was asked to collect the vegetables from the garden for the lunchtime stew. Alfred was terrified. 'My home has been destroyed…' '…my life has been ripped apart.'
Wide range of clause structures in varying position Subordinate clauses	Only Alfred, who had remained hidden, stayed alive to witness the terrifying event. As the ships drew closer, Alfred noticed the glint of swords and axes in the hands of the warriors aboard them. He laughed and laughed until he ran out of laughter.

Use of adverbs, preposition phrases and expanded noun phrases to add detail	Adverbs	Preposition phrases	Expanded noun phrases
	violently normally delicately quickly rapidly effortlessly intently suddenly only finally slowly	in a small place in the north-east of England in the kitchen Early one misty summer morning… from the garden for the lunchtime stew in the hands of the warriors	many hostile raids the beginning of the period of savage Viking history his parents to a fever two years earlier one of the lucky ones the St Cuthbert's Monks of Lindisfarne the garden for the lunchtime stew the water's edge first thing in the morning the sun rise above the horizon red and white sails blowing in the wind, floating delicately over the water the glint of swords

Commas for clarity	It was the year 793 and England was enjoying a peace that, unknown to the English, was not going to last for long.
	He was, however, one of the lucky ones, as the St Cuthbert's Monks of Lindisfarne had invited him to live with them – as long as he helped in the kitchen;
	Early one misty summer morning, Alfred was asked to collect the vegetables from the garden for the lunchtime stew.
	As he stood looking out over the horizon, he noticed what appeared to be red and white sails blowing in the wind, floating delicately over the water; it was, he thought, an enchanting sight, but how wrong could he be?
Punctuation for parenthesis	(As above for commas.)
	He was, however, one of the lucky ones, as the St Cuthbert's Monks of Lindisfarne had invited him to live with them – as long as he helped in the kitchen; and, because of their kindness, Alfred had a sense of loyalty to these old and industrious religious people.
	Sweyn Forkbeard continued to yell, 'Take what you want as your prize: gold, silver and food – anything!'
Semi-colons to mark the boundary between independent clauses	Alfred was an orphan; he had lost his parents to a fever two years earlier. He was, however, one of the lucky ones, as the St Cuthbert's Monks of Lindisfarne had invited him to live with them – as long as he helped in the kitchen; and, because of their kindness, Alfred had a sense of loyalty to these old and industrious religious people. He felt safe at Lindisfarne; it was a place where peace lived, good people prospered and happiness danced among the trees.
	As he stood looking out over the horizon, he noticed what appeared to be red and white sails blowing in the wind, floating delicately over the water; it was, he thought, an enchanting sight, but how wrong could he be?
	What he didn't realise was that this was not just beauty; it was danger…
Colons	This year marked the start of many hostile raids, hundreds of deaths and much misery: this was the beginning of the period of savage Viking history.
	'Take what you want as your prize: gold, silver and food – anything!'
	He watched them take all the gold and religious treasures, drag the sheep towards the boats and finally set light to the monastery itself: Norsemen, without conscience, without guilt, without faith.
Hyphens	cold-blooded slow-witted

5   Red

Usually, fairy tales start with 'Once upon a time' but this story is not a usual fairy tale. This tale is a true one, one that still lives on in the memory of people who knew Red. Many people have traced her footsteps and experiences to try to find the missing Red but they have never discovered her whereabouts. How do we know the story's true? Well, Red left many clues, including her bag, and her diary, which gives her account right up until the moment she vanished.

Let's start at the beginning. It's always a good place to start.

The day looked and felt normal. Red had left home at her usual time and followed her regular route. Nothing was out of place.

Red loved the very early summer sun that was streaming through the trees and warming her. It was her favourite time of day, but what Red didn't realise was that this day was to be her last one.

Sauntering through the Rainforest of Dreams, Red listened intently for the cawing of the raven and the humming of the rare Gouldian finches. Every time she followed the well-worn track she would listen in hope for the finches but had never yet heard them. Perhaps this would be her day?

The well-trodden path led towards an arch of golden light through which Red strolled to reach the ornate stone bridge. At this point, Red took her time, watching the light dance and sparkle on the river. Elegantly and expertly, kingfishers dived to catch the unsuspecting fish. She thought nature had such beauty and peace and how she loved to wander amongst it!

Daydreaming, as one does, in the Rainforest of Dreams, Red suddenly realised that she no longer knew where she was. How had she gone so wrong? She desperately cast her mind back to think about the route but couldn't remember when she had taken a wrong turning.

'I must be getting like my old grandma; she forgets things all the time,' Red noted despairingly.

Despite the heat of the rainforest, her blood froze. The trees were no longer familiar; their gnarled branches reached out across the path slowing her progress and making her feel very uncomfortable. Shadows danced mischievously, laying a false trail for her to follow. Roots of vast trees offered gateways into new worlds: worlds of mystery and fear.

Red continued cautiously, always being aware of potential danger.

In the distance, she thought she could see the outline of a city. 'I must be seeing things,' Red muttered, too loudly. 'There are no cities in the Forest of Dreams.'

As she approached the mirage, she realised that it wasn't a mirage at all, but an abandoned and ruined city. Red thought it looked like an old Aztec city: she was sure she had seen something similar in her Peruvian book. Her fear was starting to leave her and curiosity was taking its place.

Deciding to explore this undiscovered city, Red slowly wandered through the deserted streets and entered some of the darkened buildings. A cold chill seemed to live in all of the houses. People's possessions were still left on shelves and tables as if they were waiting for the owner to come home – eerie and unsettling.

Because darkness had started to descend on the city, Red wisely found a sheltered spot to light a fire and rest for the night. The fire gave a little light but inky blackness still surrounded her. Exhaustion took a hold and Red drifted into sleep: a sleep that was to be filled with shadows, fear and deception.

The shadows started to slide and sliver through the threatening blackness and across the raised, grasping roots of the trees. Rocks were swept along with the shadows; their pace increased, gaining momentum. Red suddenly felt the presence of danger closing in on her as a terrifying creature sped relentlessly towards her. She became aware of a piercing red eye watching her as if she were the prey. And of course she was. Her blood turned to ice but her hands were sweaty. With a start she woke up.

Looking around for the creature, none could be found. She was sure it was real. It had felt real.

Red was a rational and logical person. Despite feeling fear, she wasn't going to let it overcome her. Standing up, she threw her bag over her shoulder, trying desperately to feel confident, and dusted the dirt off her clothes. She set off with a sensation that things were not right but she couldn't quite put her finger on it. Something was different. The forest seemed to be watching her every move; that malice and evil was present in the air and around every corner.

'What is my problem? I'm being spooked by a nightmare. How ridiculous!' she angrily admonished herself.

An unexpected voice replied with wickedness in its heart, 'Run, Red, run! Death is near and getting closer,' it laughed, with cold malice.

The piercing red eye hung over her, immense and menacing. Red didn't need to be told twice that she should run.

Hurtling over ravines, through streams and ducking under branches that were deliberately blocking her way, Red didn't seem to gain any distance from the shadowy monster that effortlessly followed in her wake; darting here and there, changing direction made no difference.

She stumbled and fell headlong down a steep rocky slope. Luckily, she landed on her feet. Just briefly checking nothing was broken, she sprinted through a dense canopy of low growing trees and shrubs. Thorns tore at her skin. Roots caught her feet, making it difficult to move forward easily.

Suddenly and unexpectedly, the land opened out and Red stood at the edge of a precipice. There was only one way for her to go and that was across. She took a run at it and athletically flew over, landing on the other side.

She turned to see if she was being followed but there was nothing there. The previously hazardous forest now stood calmly around her, allowing shafts of light to float through the tree canopies to light up the forest floor. This image conjured up peace and security, something she hadn't felt while she was there.

She shook her head and said out loud, 'Was I imagining that? What an idiot I am!' But a whisper was heard all around her, 'I am still here, you will never shake me off.'

'Again I'm imagining things. I really mustn't eat so much cheese: it makes me hallucinate,' Red reprimanded herself once again. The whisper vanished and silence re-imposed itself.

Then, looking up, Red noticed a temple. 'I'm sure that wasn't there a minute ago.'

Curiosity is not always a good thing, as Red's mother had reminded her several times every day. Red was always asking questions, wandering off to go and investigate, eventually ending up in trouble. One day Red had found a cave that reached for many miles under the hills. With her unreliable torch, she went to investigate but got horrendously lost, her torch failed and it took three days to find her way out. Her mother hoped that this was the end of Red's idiotic adventures but in fact the incident only fuelled her curiosity further. All it really did was make sure that she prepared herself better for future eventualities.

What could go wrong? The sun was shining; there was not a cloud in the sky to threaten rain. The wind had dropped and nothing threatening was around. The birds were singing, which always meant that danger wasn't present, she thought…

All she could hear was the clatter of her boots on the stone steps. At the top, she turned right into a vast empty hall. Her footsteps echoed around the stone cavern.

Abruptly, the temperature dropped and the light was extinguished. Red turned to see the source of this but…

Now, the tale ends. No one has unveiled the meaning of the story nor provided a satisfactory - happy or unhappy - conclusion. Where did Red go and where is she now? We are just left alone with her memory. It has been a mystery for many years and it may be a mystery for many years to come.

Red's mother died in obscurity and loneliness. Sadly, she had to live with not knowing the fate of her only daughter. Perhaps time will provide a solution to the mystery and allow us to discover what really happened to Red when 'the light was extinguished'?

Analyse the text

Table 5.1

Criteria	Examples from the text	
Paragraphs to organise ideas		
Describe setting and character to create atmosphere		
Cohesive devices within and across sentences and paragraphs (including adverbials, determiners, conjunctions, pronouns and ellipses)		
Different verb forms		
Co-ordinating and subordinating conjunctions	Co-ordinating	Subordinating
Full stops and capital letters		

(continued)

Table 5.1 (*cont.*)

Question marks	
Exclamation marks	
Commas for a list of actions	
Apostrophes for contractions	
Apostrophes for possession	
Integrating dialogue (inverted commas)	
Selecting vocabulary and grammatical structures to reflect level of formality	
Passive sentences	
Modal verbs	

Wide range of clauses in varying position Subordinate clause			
Use of adverbs, preposition phrases and expanded noun phrases to add detail	**Adverbs**	**Preposition phrases**	**Expanded noun phrases**
Commas for clarity			
Dashes for parenthesis			
Semi-colons to mark the boundary between independent clauses			
Colons			
Hyphenated words			

Teacher's notes and ideas

Sentences can start with a co-ordinating conjunction such as 'and', 'but', 'or', 'yet', 'so'. These forms can be used for literary effect if used sparingly and intentionally. This needs explaining when analysing the text with the pupils.

This story was taken from the story *Le Chaperon Rouge* (this video can be found on the Literary Shed website or YouTube) – www.literacyshed.com/chaperon-rouge.html

Before reading the story, you could listen to the audio in the video without the pictures. Ask the pupils what they think is happening in the story and get them to write their own story. Then read them *Red* followed by watching the video.

When they write their own stories, pupils can change the setting or where Red sleeps or where she goes missing or what is chasing her or a combination of these. They could add another character (one brave and one scared) to create more dialogue. There is also an opportunity to develop the description of the setting further.

This is a chance to look at comparative *Little Red Riding Hood* stories and then extend the idea further by comparing with other fairy tales. They could then choose a different fairy tale to be modernised for older children. They could make it into a horror story and leave it on a cliffhanger.

Structure of the story

1 Red enters the wood – happy and relaxed
2 Finds the ruins
3 Sets up camp
4 Dreams about the shadow wolf
5 Sets off
6 Being chased
7 Arrives at deserted temple
8 Something happens (cliffhanger) and Red goes missing
9 The mystery was never solved

Table 5.2

Criteria	Examples from the text
Paragraphs to organise ideas	(As evidenced.)
Describe setting and character to create atmosphere	The well-trodden path led towards an arch of golden light through which Red strolled to reach the ornate stone bridge. At this point, Red took her time, watching the light dance and sparkle on the river. Elegantly and expertly, kingfishers dived to catch the unsuspecting fish. She thought nature had such beauty and peace and how she loved to wander amongst it! (Change of atmosphere) – The shadows started to slide and sliver through the threatening blackness and across the raised, grasping roots of the trees. Rocks were swept along with the shadows; their pace increased, gaining momentum. Red suddenly felt the presence of danger closing in on her as a terrifying creature sped relentlessly towards her. She became aware of a piercing red eye watching her as if she were the prey. And of course she was. Her blood turned to ice but her hands were sweaty. With a start she woke up.

Cohesive devices within and across sentences and paragraphs (including adverbials, determiners, conjunctions, pronouns and ellipses)	but <u>this</u> story is not a usual fairy tale <u>that</u> still lives on in the memory of the people who knew Red. <u>they</u> reached out across the path ('they' refers back to the branches) <u>it's</u> always a good place to start. ('it's' refers back to the start of the story) (See conjunctions below.)	
Different verb forms	Modal verbs (see below) had never heard have followed start '...you will never shake me off.' turned	
Co-ordinating and subordinating conjunctions	**Co-ordinating**	**Subordinating**
	and but for	which that despite because as if while
Full stops and capital letters	(As evidenced.)	
Question marks	How do we know the story's true? 'What is my problem?...' 'Was I imagining that?...' What could go wrong?	
Exclamation marks	She thought nature had such beauty and peace and how she loved to wander amongst it! '...What an idiot I am!' 'Run, Red, run!...' '...How ridiculous!'	
Commas for a list of actions	Deciding to explore this undiscovered city, Red slowly wandered through the deserted streets and entered some of the darkened buildings. Standing up, she threw her bag over her shoulder, trying desperately to feel confident, and dusted the dirt of her clothes.	
Apostrophes for contractions	wasn't I'm mustn't didn't hadn't	couldn't it's haven't let's
Apostrophes for possession	people's Red's	

(*continued*)

Table 5.2 (*cont.*)

Integrating dialogue (inverted commas)	'I must be getting like my old grandma; she forgets things all the time.' Red noted despairingly.
	'I must be seeing things,' Red muttered, too loudly.
	'There are no cities in the Forest of Dreams.'
	'What is my problem? I'm being spooked by a nightmare. How ridiculous!' she angrily admonished herself.
	'Run, Red, run! Death is near and getting closer,' it laughed, with cold malice.
	'Was I imagining that? What an idiot I am!'
	But a whisper was heard all around her, 'I am still here, you will never shake me off.'
	'Again I'm imagining things. I really mustn't eat so much cheese: it makes me hallucinate,' Red reprimanded herself once again.
	'I'm sure that wasn't there a minute ago.'
Selecting vocabulary and grammatical structures to reflect level of formality	Powerful verbs: traced, discovered, including, streaming
	Warming, sauntering, cawing, humming, strolled, daydreaming, noted, continued, muttered, approached, descend, sheltered, drifted, sliver, hurtling, stumbled, conjured up, vanished, reminded, extinguished, unveiled
	Adjectives: regular, well-worn, well-trodden, ornate, unsuspecting, gnarled, potential, outline, abandoned, ruined, undiscovered, deserted, darkened, eerie, unsettling, sheltered, inky, threatening, piercing, unexpected, immense, menacing, shadowy, dense, hazardous, shafts of, unreliable, horrendously
	Adverbs: intently, elegantly, expertly, desperately, despairingly, mischievously, relentlessly, desperately, deliberately, effortlessly, briefly, unexpectedly, athletically, previously, horrendously, abruptly
	Nouns: memory, experiences, whereabouts, account, curiosity, possessions, blackness, exhaustion, deception, momentum, sensation, malice, wickedness, ravines, canopy, security, footsteps, solution
Passive sentences	Just briefly checking nothing was broken…
	She turned to see if she was being followed…
Modal verbs	would, could, should, must, will,
Wide range of clauses and varying positions Subordinate clause	Despite feeling fear, she wasn't going to let it overcome her. The well-trodden path led towards an arch of golden light through which Red strolled to reach the ornate stone bridge.

Use of adverbs, pre-position phrases and expanded noun phrases to add detail	Adverbs	Preposition phrases	Expanded noun phrases
	intently	with her memory	an arch of golden light through which Red strolled to reach the ornate stone bridge
	elegantly	with cold malice	
	expertly	with wickedness	
	desperately	at the beginning	the missing Red
	despairingly	at her usual time	the beginning
	mischievously	through the threatening blackness	the cawing of the raven
	relentlessly		the rare Gouldian finches
	desperately	through the deserted streets	the unsuspecting fish
	deliberately		the outline of a city
	effortlessly	amongst it	the shadowy monster that effortlessly followed in her wake
	briefly	in its heart	
	unexpectedly	in the memory of people who knew Red	
	athletically		
	previously	in the Rainforest of Dreams	
	horrendously	at this point	
	abruptly	across the path	
		into new worlds	
		in the distance	
Commas for clarity	This tale is a true one, one that still lives on in the memory of people who knew Red. Sauntering through the Rainforest of Dreams, Red listened intently for the cawing of the raven and the humming of the rare Gouldian finches. At this point, Red took her time, watching the light dance and sparkle on the river. Daydreaming, as one does, in the Rainforest of Dreams, Red suddenly realised that she no longer knew where she was. Red continued cautiously, always being aware of potential danger. Suddenly and unexpectedly, the land opened out and Red stood at the edge of a precipice. She took a run at it and athletically flew over, landing on the other side. Standing up, she threw her bag over her shoulder, trying desparately to feel confident, and dusted the dirt off her clothes.		
Dashes for parenthesis	People's possessions were still left on shelves and tables as if they were waiting for the owner to come home – eerie and unsettling. No one has unveiled the meaning of the story nor provided a satisfactory – happy or unhappy – conclusion.		

(*continued*)

Table 5.2 (*cont.*)

Semi-colons to mark the boundary between independent clauses	'I must be getting like my old grandma; she forgets things all the time,' Red noted despairingly. The trees were no longer familiar; their gnarled branches reached out across the path, slowing her progress and making her feel very uncomfortable. Rocks were swept along with the shadows; their pace increased, gaining momentum. The forest seemed to be watching her every move; that malice and evil was present in the air and around every corner. Red didn't seem to gain any distance from the shadowy monster that effortlessly followed in her wake; darting here and there, changing direction made no difference. The sun was shining; there was not a cloud in the sky to threaten rain.
Colons	Roots of vast trees offered gateways into new worlds: worlds of mystery and fear. Red thought it looked like an old Aztec city: she was sure she had seen something similar in her Peruvian book. Exhaustion took a hold and Red drifted into sleep: a sleep that was to be filled with shadows, fear and deception. 'Again I'm imagining things. I really mustn't eat so much cheese: it makes me hallucinate,' Red reprimanded herself once again.
Hyphenated words	well-worn re-imposed well-trodden

6   The Blitz

A year ago today, I was sent to the countryside to be safe and avoid the bombing that everyone said was coming, but it never came – and I hated my host family so I ran away. My escape was made difficult because there was little transport as petrol was rationed; the government, for the war effort, had confiscated many vehicles and the use of petrol was prioritised for the armed forces.

However, it wasn't long after I arrived home that the Blitz actually started. Luckily for me, my school received a direct hit from a well-aimed German bomber. Thank you Mr German for demolishing the school, which meant that all lessons were cancelled, and probably, for a very long time.

I was very lonely as all my friends had stayed in the countryside but I managed to occupy myself by playing in the bombed-out buildings. Most of the time I could lose myself in the adventures I had created, but every now and then, I would be reminded that these ruined buildings had once been lived in happily by real people. One day I found a picture frame with a photo of a rather serious-looking mother, a stern father and three well-behaved children staring into the camera. It made me wonder about the family, their whereabouts now, who they were and whether they were still alive – and that made me feel even more lonely.

On one of these days, as I was scrambling up a mountain of rubble, the air raid siren started to wail. Slowly, at first, with frightening authority, until it built up its momentum into a compulsive series of wails that couldn't be ignored.

Strangely, the skies were silent but then, through the grey clouds, a persistent hum could be heard. This was followed by an arrowhead formation of German planes, which swarmed into sight like a scourge of mosquitoes. The planes' humming grew louder and louder until it was deafening. I was transfixed by the combined sound of screaming sirens and the hypnotic drone of the planes. I couldn't move. Frozen, I was, just frozen.

Then, sprinting round the corner, came an ARP warden, waving his torch and blowing his whistle. He ran past me shouting, 'Go to the closest air raid shelter sonny, now!'

I don't know why, but I couldn't seem to respond. I was paralysed by the noise and mesmerised by the panic-stricken crowd who were scurrying and flailing around. Yet, everyone seemed to have a purpose, a mission, a destination. Mine was to be a bad move, a really bad move as I was to find out soon enough.

As suddenly as they appeared, the planes released their deadly cargo. First they dropped the incendiary bombs to light up London with fires and then the great bombers appeared and released the big and more devastating bombs on their now visible targets.

Fires sprung up all around the London streets and the smoke choked and blinded me. I stumbled and fell clumsily down the pile of rubble, scratching and bruising every part of my body. For a moment, I fell unconscious but recovered when I heard people shouting and felt the heat from the fires raging close by.

Through the dim light, I could see boots trampling past me. I spotted firewatchers carrying dustbin lids. I thought this was a bit silly but then realised that they used them as heat shields when fighting to extinguish the firebombs.

Two men were holding on to one hosepipe, which was having very little effect on the roaring flames. The bombs just kept coming: falling, falling relentlessly, but despite the incessant bombings, the firefighters just fought on. It seemed like hell had been invited to a devil's revel over London.

The fires spread everywhere, jumping from house to house, leaving just the skeleton of the buildings silhouetted starkly against the raging red sky. It was time to run. It was time to find safety from the hell that was surrounding me.

I ran in any direction; I didn't know where I was going. The streets were collapsing around me, being violently dismantled by bomb, after bomb, after bomb. I could no longer recognise my own home town. I just knew that I needed to escape – to get away from the suffocating heat and smoke of the fires and the fury. But where could I go?

Racing down the High Street, I came to a sudden halt as I nearly ran straight into a coil of barbed wire. There was no way forward. I glanced behind and made for the side street. Then, unfortunately, I ran straight into a dead-end lane! Just the wrong place!

For a brief moment, there was silence and then the onslaught continued. The Luftwaffe threw down their deadly bombs without any care for life. I turned to go back but a massive bomb landed on the opposite side of the street and brought down the Old Post Office. I threw myself to the ground: dust and rubble rained down on me. I was hurt.

The pain was immense. I lay there for a while waiting for the next attack but nothing happened. I pulled myself out of the rubble and watched the dust gently float down. I could see nothing, I could hear nothing but, as the dust slowly cleared, the reality emerged. It was horrendous. I could see parts of bodies reaching out from under red bricks, sheets of metal and household items. As my vision cleared, in the centre of the road I could see a massive hole with a bus protruding from it.

Just as I was starting to comprehend the chaos, another bomb screamed down and hit the street running parallel to mine. Yet another explosion reached for the sky and then it all seemed to happen in slow motion. Debris was spread far and wide. Frozen to the spot, I just watched as people shouted and ran around saving anyone who was lucky enough to survive: anyone who had a hope, who was fighting for life.

I could hear people screaming and wailing above the sound of the fire engine bell. The hurt that exploded from their despair will live with me forever.

I'm not sure I was really aware when the all-clear siren sounded but I do know the bombing had eventually ceased. Even though it was the end of the bombing for that night, I knew it would come again and again; it certainly wasn't the end. Every time the siren sounded to show the end of another night's bombing, it brought with it both good and, inevitably, bad news.

With a sorrowful heart, I quietly watched people emerge, shaken and confused, from their shelters. I wondered what each person's story would be and how many of us would still be alive tomorrow to fight another wicked Blitz.

We are determined not to give in; how can we?

Yet, out of the horror, I felt a strange spirit stirring in my soul. Bravery and determination surrounded me as I stood there, among the ruins. The blitzed and bewildered people who emerged from their shelters had not given in. They were standing up to fight another day.

They were not going to accept defeat: now or ever. It was the Blitz that was going to be defeated.

I stepped over the rubble and joined the throng of people returning home. Not knowing what they were going to be confronted with.

Analyse the text

Table 6.1

Criteria	Examples from the text	
Summary of each paragraph		
Describe setting and character to create atmosphere		
Cohesive devices within and across sentences and paragraphs (including adverbials, determiners, conjunctions, pronouns and ellipses)		
Different verb forms used accurately		
Co-ordinating and subordinating conjunctions	**Co-ordinating**	**Sub-ordinating**
Question marks		
Exclamation marks		
Commas for lists		
Apostrophes for contraction		
Selecting vocabulary and grammatical structure to reflect the level of formality		

(continued)

Table 6.1 (*cont.*)

Passive sentences	
Modal verbs	
Wide range of clause structures in varying position Subordinate clauses	
Adverbs	
Preposition phrases	
Expanded noun phrases	
Inverted commas	
Commas for clarity	
Semi-colons to mark the boundary between independent clauses	
Hyphens	
Wide range of punctuation	
Colons to mark the boundary between independent clauses	

Teacher's notes and ideas

This story will be more effective if you have taught about evacuation and why a little boy would return from the countryside to live back in London.

One exercise for the pupils would be to find one picture for each paragraph on the internet. Or you can ask the pupils to say in no more than five words what each paragraph is about. This shows them that each paragraph should be about one thing.

Play the air raid siren warning at the beginning and then the all-clear siren at the end (www.bbc.co.uk/schoolradio/subjects/history/ww2clips).

This structure could lead into a poem using figurative language (see poetry section). Pull out words and phrases that could be used in the poem. Teach the figurative language you want to include such as metaphors, personification or similes. The poem follows the structure of the story.

The pupils could act out the story. Use drama conventions/strategies for the pupils to empathise with the character (http://dramaresource.com/drama-strategies/).

Another idea would be to find out more about the character. The pupils create the backstory of the character. What is he like? No name has been given so it gives the pupils complete licence to create their own ideas. Use the clues from the story to help.

There are many YouTube clips showing London during the Blitz demonstrating what it was like for those that lived there then.

Another option would be to write a discussion on whether it was more exciting to live in the city now or during the Blitz.

To collect vocabulary and develop sentences, find pictures of London during the Blitz (an excellent book for photographs is *Images of World War II (Photographs from the Daily Mail)*; ISBN – 1-40544-895-4). Stick the photographs in the centre of a large piece of paper and ask the pupils to walk round the room and write the nouns/abstract nouns they see, then adjectives, verbs and adverbs around the outside of the picture. Build up different sentence constructions using the vocabulary collected.

Sentences can start with a co-ordinating conjunction such as 'and', 'but', 'or', 'yet', 'so'. These forms can be used for literary effect if used sparingly and intentionally. This needs explaining when analysing the text with the pupils.

Structure of the story

1 Boy playing on a bomb site
2 The air raid siren goes off
3 Experiences the incendiary bombs
4 Watches firemen trying to put the fires out
5 Gets lost and can't find a shelter (more bombs are dropped, gets caught up in the barbed wire and prevented from proceeding by the mountain of rubble)
6 The all-clear siren goes off
7 Sees people emerge from the shelters and has thoughts about the future

Table 6.2

Criteria	Examples from the text
Summary of each paragraph	1 Ran away from host family
	2 School demolished because of the Blitz
	3 Playing on own
	4 Air siren goes off
	5 The approaching bombers
	6 ARP shouts instructions

Table 6.2 (*cont.*)

	7 Stood watching what is happening 8 Incendiary bombs 9 Injured himself 10–12 The fires 13 Running to find shelter 14 Trapped 15–17 The bomb and its aftermath 18 All-clear siren 19 People emerging from the shelter
Describe setting and character to create atmosphere	Strangely, the skies were silent but then, through the grey clouds, a persistent hum could be heard. This was followed by an arrowhead formation of German planes, which swarmed into sight like a scourge of mosquitoes. The planes' humming grew louder and louder until it was deafening. I was transfixed by the combined sound of screaming sirens and the hypnotic drone of the planes. I couldn't move. Frozen, I was, just frozen. The fires spread everywhere, jumping from house to house, leaving just the skeleton of the buildings silhouetted starkly against the raging red sky. It was time to run. It was time to find safety from the hell that was surrounding me. I ran in any direction; I didn't know where I was going. The streets were collapsing around me, being violently dismantled by bomb, after bomb, after bomb. I could no longer recognise my own home town.
Cohesive devices	<u>the</u> air raid siren started to wail. <u>Slowly, at first</u>, with frightening authority, <u>until it</u> built up its momentum into a compulsive series of wails…
Different verb forms used accurately	I <u>was</u> very lonely as all my friends <u>had stayed</u> in the countryside but I <u>managed to occupy myself</u> by <u>playing</u> in the bombed-out buildings. Most of the time I <u>could lose myself</u> in the adventures I <u>had created</u>, but every now and then, I <u>would be reminded</u> that these ruined buildings <u>had once been lived in</u> happily by real people. One day I <u>found</u> a picture frame with a photo of a rather serious-looking mother, a stern father and three well-behaved children <u>staring</u> into the camera. It <u>made</u> <u>me wonder about</u> the family, their whereabouts now, who they <u>were</u> and whether they <u>were</u> still alive – and that <u>made</u> me feel even more lonely. We <u>are determined not to give in</u>; how <u>can</u> we? (Present and infinitive form) The hurt that <u>exploded</u> from their despair <u>will live</u> with me forever. (Future tense)
Co-ordinating and subor-dinating conjunctions	And, but, so Which, until, despite, whether, as
Question marks	We are determined not to give in; how can we? …where could I go?
Exclamation marks	He ran past me shouting, 'Go to the closest air raid shelter, now!'
Commas for lists	Then, sprinting round the corner, came an ARP warden, waving his torch and blowing his whistle. One day I found a picture frame with a photo of a rather serious-looking mother, a stern father and three well-behaved children staring into the camera.

Apostrophes for contraction	wasn't couldn't don't	didn't I'm
Selecting vocabulary and grammatical structure to reflect the level of formality	As suddenly as they appeared, the planes released their deadly cargo. (A sense of urgency and speed, starting with a simile.) We are determined not to give in; how can we? (Use of first person plural to show how London is united. Move from formality to informality by asking a tag question.) A year ago today, I was sent to the countryside to be safe and avoid the bombing that everyone said was coming, but it never came – and I hated my host family so I ran away. My escape was made difficult because there was little transport as petrol was rationed; (Begins with first person informal) the government, for the war effort, had confiscated many vehicles and the use of petrol was prioritised for the armed forces. (The latter part is formal, explaining historical fact.)	
Passive	My escape was made difficult… …petrol was rationed… …petrol was prioritised…	
Modal verbs	would, could, can, will	
Wide range of clause structures in varying position Subordinate clauses	This was followed by an arrowhead formation of German planes, which swarmed into sight like a scourge of mosquitoes. On one of these days, as I was scrambling up a mountain of rubble, the air raid siren started to wail. The planes' humming grew louder and louder until it was deafening. The bombs just kept coming: falling, falling relentlessly, but despite the incessant bombings, the firefighters just fought on.	
Adverbs	luckily for me once everywhere violently nearly unfortunately gently slowly really eventually certainly inevitably quietly	actually probably happily slowly strangely really suddenly clumsily relentlessly starkly every now and then
Preposition phrases	a year ago today for the armed forces from a well-aimed German bomber in the bombed-out buildings most of the time by real people into the camera with frightening authority for a very long time.	with frightening authority for a very long time into a compulsive series of wails that couldn't be ignored by the combined sound of screaming sirens and the hypnotic drone of the planes for a moment

(continued)

Table 6.2 (*cont.*)

Expanded noun phrases	these ruined buildings had once been lived in happily by real people a picture frame with a photo of a rather serious-looking mother, a stern father and three well-behaved children the heights of a rubble mountain a wail that was hard to ignore the pile of rubble a direct hit from a well-aimed German bomber all my friends the combined sound of screaming sirens and the hypnotic drone of the planes the incendiary bombs to light up London with fires the skeleton of the buildings silhouetted starkly against the raging red sky
Inverted commas	He ran past me shouting, 'Go to the closest air raid shelter, now!'
Commas for clarity	However, it wasn't long after I arrived home that the Blitz actually started. Thank you Mr German for demolishing the school, which meant that all lessons were cancelled, and probably, for a very long time. Most of the time I could lose myself in the adventures I had created, but every now and then, I would be reminded that… Slowly, at first, with frightening authority, until it built up its momentum into a compulsive series of wails that couldn't be ignored. Frozen, I was, just frozen. Mine was to be a bad move, a really bad move as I was to find out soon enough.
Semi-colon to mark the boundary between independent clauses	My escape was made difficult because there was little transport as petrol was rationed; the government, for the war effort, had confiscated many vehicles and the use of petrol was prioritised for the armed forces. I ran in any direction; I didn't know where I was going. Even though it was the end of the bombing for that night, I knew it would come again and again; it certainly wasn't the end. We are determined not to give in; how can we?
Hyphens	well-aimed　　　　　　　　　panic-stricken bombed-out　　　　　　　　　all-clear well-behaved
Wide range of punctuation	Full stops, inverted commas, commas, colons, semi-colons, hyphens
Colons to mark the boundary between independent clauses	The bombs just kept coming: falling, falling relentlessly, but despite the incessant bombings, the firefighters just fought on. I threw myself to the ground: dust and rubble rained down on me. Frozen to the spot, I just watched as people shouted and ran around saving anyone who was lucky enough to survive: anyone who had a hope, who was fighting for life. They were not going to accept defeat: now or ever.

7   The Myth of Osiris and Isis

As with much of the Ancient Egyptian mythology, there are various versions of the story of Isis and Osiris, but basically it runs as follows...

Osiris, an Egyptian God who was the son of Geb and Nut, ruled over ancient Egypt with his wife Isis. He was a popular king with his subjects but, unfortunately, this popularity angered his brother, Set.

Anger turned into jealously for Set so he plotted to rid the land of Osiris by using trickery to kill him. This would leave the path clear for Set to become king and ruler of a vast land: a land that reached from the ocean to the heartland mountains and crossed lakes and deserts to its capital city, where its culture inspired the world with its art and architecture.

Set's plans to dispose of his brother started to materialise when he secretly obtained Osiris's measurements and designed a majestic casket which would only fit Osiris. The casket was in the form of a human-shaped box, skilfully carved to enclose the body of Osiris. It was bejewelled with precious stones and enamelled with lapis lazuli interspersed with pure gold: a casket befitting a king.

Set then organised a large feast, to which Osiris and a number of other important guests were invited. At the height of the festivities, Set produced the casket and announced that it would be given to whomsoever it fitted.

'This magnificent casket is a present to anyone who is worthy of greatness: a greatness that will give you a direct pathway to heaven. Who will try it for size?' Set asked the spellbound guests.

The richness of the casket reached into the hearts of the other guests and many of them longed to possess such an impressive object. Desire joined greed to form a river that raced through the guests' thoughts.

'This is mine,' one over-hopeful guest whispered hoarsely to another startled guest.

'You are not great enough!' the startled guest retorted. 'I'm more important than you!'

All of them desperately tried the casket for size but it fitted no one, until finally Osiris stepped into the casket. It fitted perfectly. Well, are we surprised at that?

Set immediately slammed the lid closed and sealed it shut tightly. The guests were so shocked that they immediately fled, fearing that they would suffer the same fate. The sealed coffin was then thrown into the Nile to be lost forever.

However, Set misjudged the power of love. Isis was devastated at the death of her husband. Set did not realise that Isis's love for her husband and her desire for a child would drive her to search the distant lands for him until she found him. She feared that without the proper ceremony, Osiris would not be able to reach the place of the dead and be properly judged at the gate to heaven: his heart would never be weighed against the feather of truth to evidence all his good deeds.

Also, for many years, she had longed for a child to produce the next king of Egypt but for many years no child had been given to them. Isis realised that she would have to seek out Osiris's body. This would allow her to breathe new life into Osiris, just for as long as a child could be produced and, after that, he would then receive a funeral fit for a king. With the help of her sister Nephthys, Set's wife, she searched for the casket throughout Egypt and across many lands and many countries. It took her years and years but she eventually found it resting in the roots of a massive Cedar tree, which now held up the palace of Byblos.

The king of Byblos willingly gave the coffin to Isis; now she could travel back to Egypt with her husband's body. On her return, she concealed it in the marshes beside the Nile for safekeeping because she knew Set would attempt to steal the body again if he knew it was once again in Egypt – his desire to rule was so great that nothing would stop him. Unfortunately for Isis, her hiding place was to be discovered. Set found the casket while out hunting and he was so enraged he chopped the body of Osiris into 14 pieces and scattered the parts throughout the kingdom. Each part represented one of the 14 full moons in a year.

Set knew – or thought – that now it'd be impossible for Isis to find the body and bring Osiris back to life.

'Isis has underestimated me and my powers. This time Osiris will stay dead for always,' Set laughed cruelly. His laughter echoed throughout the vastness of the universe and turned the blood of his listeners cold: but for just a brief moment.

Isis, however, determined and resolute, set out to prove Set wrong. She knew the journey would be dangerous and might, again, take many years but she also knew that it could and must be done. Eventually, after overcoming many hazards and torments, she found all the parts except one. With the re-found parts, she reassembled Osiris, and wrapped him carefully in bandages. Unfortunately, the fourteenth part had been eaten by a fish so she re-fashioned and replaced the missing part in gold. The body was complete.

Now, possessing the reassembled body, Isis breathed renewed life back into Osiris and it was then that they conceived a child and named him Horus – the future king of Egypt.

After the child was born, Isis could bury her husband and allow him to travel to the land of the dead. On arriving at the land of the dead, Osiris – once a great God and king – was made Lord of the Dead and Afterlife (sometimes also known as the underworld). He presided over the 'weighing of the heart' ceremony, which determined if people were worthy enough to enter the afterlife.

He had, at last, finally come to rest after so many years of living between the two worlds, earth and the afterlife.

It was now inevitable that Horus would have to fight Set to decide, finally, who should be the new ruler of Egypt: but this is another myth for another time and it is a myth which also has many different versions...

Analyse the text

Table 7.1

Criteria	Examples from the text	
Describe setting and character to create atmosphere		
Cohesive devices within and across sentences and paragraphs (including adverbials, determiners, conjunctions, pronouns and ellipses)		
Different verb forms		
Co-ordinating and subordinating conjunctions	**Co-ordinating**	**Subordinating**
Question marks		
Exclamation marks		
Apostrophes for contractions		
Apostrophes for possession		

(continued)

Table 7.1 (*cont.*)

Creating atmosphere and integrating dialogue to convey action and character			
Selecting vocabulary and grammatical structure reflecting the level of formality			
Modal verbs			
Passive sentences			
Wide range of clause structures in varying position Subordinate clauses			
Use of adverbs, preposition phrases and expanded noun phrases to add detail	Adverbs	Preposition phrases	Expanded noun phrases

Inverted commas	
Commas for clarity	
Punctuation for parenthesis	
Semi-colons to mark the boundary between independent clauses	
Colons	
Hyphens	
Dashes	
Managing shifts between levels of formality	

Teacher's notes and ideas

1 The pupils could draw out the story in cartoon version.
2 Challenge the pupils to write the story in less than 300 words, 150 words and 50 words.
3 Compare with other myths.
4 Compare with other versions of the story.
5 Stop at certain parts of the story to see what the pupils would suggest. For example: '*Set's plans to dispose of his brother started to materialise when he secretly obtained Osiris's measurements...*' What do the pupils think Set will do with the measurements?
6 Which parts could be part of a real story and which parts could never have happened?
7 Why was this story told?
8 How else could Set have rid himself of his brother?
9 There is a chance to explore the consequences of jealousy and how it ruins people's lives.

Structure of the story

1 Introduction of the characters Set and Osiris and an overview of the plot to kill the king using a trick.
2 At the party, Set challenges the guests to try the casket, including Osiris. When Osiris climbs in, Set seals it and throws it into the Nile.
3 Isis sets out to look for Osiris's body because without a proper burial he would not go to the place of the dead.
4 She learnt that the coffin had been embedded in a tree.
5 After finding the coffin, Isis hid it in the marshland by the River Nile.
6 Set found the coffin and dismembered the body into 14 parts to scatter around Egypt.
7 Isis had to look for all the body parts. She only found 13 parts; the fourteenth part had been eaten. Isis made the missing part out of gold.
8 Osiris was resurrected and then buried properly.
9 Osiris became Lord of the Dead and the Afterlife.

Table 7.2

Criteria	Examples from the text
Describe setting and character to create atmosphere	Anger turned into jealously for Set so he plotted to rid the land of Osiris by using trickery to kill him. This would leave the path clear for Set to become king and ruler of a vast land: a land that reached from the ocean to the heartland mountains and crossed lakes and deserts to its capital city, where its culture inspired the world with its art and architecture.
	Set's plans to dispose of his brother started to materialise when he secretly obtained Osiris's measurements and designed a majestic casket which would only fit Osiris. The casket was in the form of a human-shaped box, skilfully carved to enclose the body of Osiris. It was bejewelled with precious stones and enamelled with lapis lazuli interspersed with pure gold: a casket befitting a king.
	With the help of her sister Nephthys, Set's wife, she searched for the casket throughout Egypt and across many lands and many countries. It took her years and years but she eventually found it resting in the roots of a massive Cedar tree, which now held up the palace of Byblos.

Cohesive devices within and across sentences and paragraphs (including adverbials, determiners, conjunctions, pronouns and ellipses)	<u>whomsoever</u> it fitted <u>this</u> time <u>that</u> it would be given <u>his</u> subjects <u>her</u> husband <u>after</u> the child was born (See also conjunctions, adverbs and preposition phrases below.)	
Different verb forms	are ruled to rid using would would be given	will give had longed had been given had been eaten has underestimated would have to seek out
Co-ordinating and subordinating conjunctions	Co-ordinating and but so for	Subordinating when until after because that if
Question marks	'…Who will try it for size?' Well, are we surprised at that?	
Exclamation marks	'You are not great enough!' 'I'm more important than you!'	
Apostrophes for contractions	I'm it'd	
Apostrophes for possession	Osiris's Set's guests'	Isis's husband's
Creating atmosphere and integrating dialogue to convey action and character	The richness of the casket reached into the hearts of the other guests and many of them longed to possess such an impressive object. Desire joined greed to form a river that raced through the guests' thoughts. 'This is mine,' one over-hopeful guest whispered hoarsely to another startled guest. 'You are not great enough!' the startled guest retorted. 'I'm more important than you!' All of them desperately tried the casket for size but it fitted no one, until finally Osiris stepped into the casket. It fitted perfectly. Well, are we surprised at that? (The dialogue reinforces the expense and desirability of the casket by being given access to the guests' thoughts.)	

(*continued*)

Table 7.2 (*cont.*)

Selecting vocabulary and grammatical structure reflecting the level of formality	Written in the third person – she/he. Past tense as this is a story which happened thousands of years ago. Chronological. Technical (Egyptian vocabulary) – casket instead of coffin. Speech reflects the authority of the person – 'This magnificent casket is a present to anyone who is worthy of greatness: a greatness that will give you a direct pathway to heaven. Who will try it for size?' Set asked the spellbound guests. Vocabulary is formal to reflect the myth.
Modal verbs	could, should, would, will, must
Passive sentences	…no child had been given to them… Unfortunately, the fourteenth part had been eaten by a fish…
Wide range of clause structures in varying position Subordinate clauses	Set's plans to dispose of his brother started to materialise when he secretly obtained Osiris's measurements and designed a majestic casket which would only fit Osiris. After the child was born, Isis could bury her husband and allow him to travel to the land of the dead. Osiris, an Egyptian God who was the son of Geb and Nut, ruled over ancient Egypt with his wife Isis. All of them desperately tried the casket for size but it fitted no one, until finally Osiris stepped into the casket.

Use of adverbs, preposition phrases and expanded noun phrases to add detail	Adverbs	Preposition phrases	Expanded noun phrases
	as with much of the Ancient Egyptian mythology basically unfortunately jealously secretly only skilfully hoarsely finally tightly immediately desperately perfectly properly eventually willingly cruelly eventually carefully unfortunately	at the height of the festivities on arriving at the land of the dead with precious stones and enamelled with lapis lazuli interspersed with pure gold with its art and architecture throughout Egypt and across many lands and many countries throughout the vastness of the universe in the form of a human-shaped box into the hearts of the other guests	lapis lazuli interspersed with pure gold a large feast, to which Osiris and a number of other important guests were invited this enriched casket a greatness that will give you a direct pathway to heaven the richness of the casket her desire for a child new life into Osiris

Inverted commas	'This magnificent casket is a present to anyone who is worthy of greatness: a greatness that will give you a direct pathway to heaven. Who will try it for size?' Set asked the spellbound guests. 'This is mine,' one over-hopeful guest whispered hoarsely to another startled guest. 'You are not great enough!' the startled guest retorted. 'I'm more important than you!' 'Isis has underestimated me and my powers. This time Osiris will stay dead for always,'
Commas for clarity	Osiris, an Egyptian God who was the son of Geb and Nut, ruled over ancient Egypt with his wife Isis. At the height of the festivities, Set produced the casket and announced that it would be given to whomsoever it fitted. She feared that without the proper ceremony, Osiris would not be able to reach the place of the dead and be properly judged at the gate to heaven: his heart would never be weighed against the feather of truth to evidence all his good deeds. With the help of her sister Nephthys, Set's wife, she searched for the casket throughout Egypt and across many lands and many countries. With the re-found parts, she reassembled Osiris, and wrapped him carefully in bandages.
Punctuation for parenthesis	(See *Commas for clarity* above as well.) Now, possessing the reassembled body, Isis breathed renewed life back into Osiris and it was then that they conceived a child and named him Horus – the future king of Egypt. Set knew – or thought – that now it'd be impossible for Isis to find the body and bring Osiris back to life. On arriving at the land of the dead, Osiris – once a great God and king – was made Lord of the Dead and Afterlife (sometimes also known as the underworld).
Semi-colons to mark the the boundary between independ-ent clauses	The king of Byblos willingly gave the coffin to Isis; now she could travel back to Egypt with her husband's body.

(*continued*)

Table 7.2 (*cont.*)

Colons	This would leave the path clear for Set to become king and ruler of a vast land: a land that reached from the ocean to the heartland mountains and crossed lakes and deserts to its capital city, where its culture inspired the world with its art and architecture.
	It was bejewelled with precious stones and enamelled with lapis lazuli interspersed with pure gold: a casket befitting a king.
	'This magnificent casket is a present to anyone who is worthy of greatness: a greatness that will give you a direct pathway to heaven…'
	Set immediately slammed the lid closed and sealed it: shut tightly.
	She feared that without the proper ceremony, Osiris would not be able to reach the place of the dead and be properly judged at the gate to heaven: his heart would never be weighed against the feather of truth to evidence all his good deeds.
	His laughter echoed throughout the vastness of the universe and turned the blood of his listeners cold: but for just a brief moment.
	It was now inevitable that Horus would have to fight Set to decide, finally, who should be the new ruler of Egypt: but this is another myth for another time and it is a myth which also has many different versions…
Hyphens	human-shaped
	over-hopeful
	re-found
	re-fashioned
Dashes	See *Punctuation for parenthesis* section
Managing shifts between levels of formality	(Starts with a chatty form.) – As with much of the Ancient Egyptian mythology, there are various versions of the story of Isis and Osiris, but basically it runs as follows…
	(The story then maintains the format of a myth but is briefly interspersed with a hypothetical question as the writer addresses the audience directly.) – Well are we that surprised?

PART II

Non-fiction

8   Biography of Louis Braille

Why is he famous?

Louis Braille invented a tactile alphabet for the blind. It was a system that totally changed, indeed revolutionised, the lives of multitudes of blind people by enabling them to read, simply, with the tips of their fingers: an outstanding achievement.

Childhood

Louis Braille was born on 4 January 1809 in the small town of Coupvray in France, just 20 miles east of Paris. He was the fourth child of Monique and Simon-René: his eldest sibling had been named after his mother (Monique Catherine born 1793); the second sibling, for some strange reason, had been given the same name as Louis (Louis-Simon born 1795); and the third, Marie Céline (born 1797), managed to acquire an individual name for herself.

In the early nineteenth century, Coupvray was a small, rural village with many of its inhabitants living off the land. At that time, farmers used horses to plough their fields, for personal transportation and for carrying heavy loads – unlike today where they use cars, tractors and trucks. As a result, one of the most important jobs in the village was a leather worker; this was his father's profession. He worked as a village saddler making harnesses, tack and saddles for the surrounding farms and the local gentry.

Louis had a happy childhood, spending many hours with his father in his workshop playing with the multitude of tools but it was there, in the workshop, that the unfortunate accident occurred which was to have a massive impact on Louis for the rest of his life.

How he became blind

At the age of three, while his father was busy, Louis was playing with an awl (a sharp tool which is used to punch holes in leather) but it accidentally slipped, flew out of his hand and first pierced, then punctured, his left eye. Despite being looked after by the best doctor in the area, Louis continued to be in great difficulty and agony for many months. Those months turned into years during which doctors struggled to save his eye, but bad news came when he was told that the eye had, tragically, to be removed. Even worse news came when Louis found out that the infection had spread to his right eye – and that there was no hope of saving it. So, by the time Louis was five years old, he was completely blind.

Education

To begin with, Louis attended the local school, which unfortunately did not cater for pupils who were blind. Despite being a diligent and hard-working student, he struggled to keep up with the other pupils, consequently suffering ridicule and bullying. Louis stayed at this school for five years but he simply could not learn everything just by listening. However, things improved when he won a scholarship to the Royal Institution for Blind Youth in Paris (RIBY); he was then just 10 years old. At the RIBY, Louis acquired both academic and vocational skills but, even there, most of the teachers just talked at him and the rest of the students, making learning a very difficult process.

Reading was still very challenging for him and books were not plentiful: the library only contained 14 huge books with raised letters, which made for very hard and slow reading. These books were written in a Latin script that was raised above the page so that blind readers could follow the text by using their fingers: this was known as the Haüy system, invented by Valentine Haüy (the founder of the RIBY). This system was slow, and Louis was impatient: he wanted to read quickly and he wanted to read extensively.

How he invented the Braille system

His impatience motivated Louis to seek, and eventually find, an alternative way for blind people to read.

This opportunity came in 1821, when a former soldier named Charles Barbier de la Serre, a captain in the French army, visited the school. Barbier presented his invention, called 'night writing', which incorporated a code of 12 raised dots and dashes that allowed soldiers to share top-secret information on the battlefield without having to speak or, at night, use a light (night lights were dangerous and, perilously, revealed their positions to the enemy). Unfortunately, the code was too complicated for the soldiers and therefore was neither developed nor used as a military tool. However, the important upshot was that this experience inspired and motivated 12-year-old Louis to improve the Barbier system.

With great excitement, he spent hours, days and years simplifying and adapting a version of Barbier's idea. Louis reduced Barbier's 12-dot system to six: three dots lined up in each of two columns in a cell no larger than a fingertip. He assigned different combinations of dots to different letters and punctuation marks, with a total of 64 symbols.

Even though the system allowed blind people to read and write easily and quickly, it remained controversial for many years.

In an attempt to reach out to the blind community, Louis published the first-ever braille book in 1829, but it was very quickly criticised and rejected, predominantly by sighted people. Braille needed to prove that the method had value, so he taught other blind pupils to read using the six-dot system. Despite its popularity with the blind community, the teachers would not and could not see its validity. The only champion of the new method was the school's director, Alexandre François-René Pignier, but after he was forced to retire in 1840, the next director, Pierre-Armand Dufau, banned Braille's new system altogether. This meant that it vanished into obscurity. Facing such public doubt, blind students were forced to study the Braille system secretly and in their own time, even at the Royal Institute where Braille worked.

Adult life

At the age of 19, after leaving school, Louis became an apprentice teacher at the RIBY, and five years later he was offered a full professorship to teach history, geometry and algebra.

A strong and continued belief in his invention inspired Braille to publish another book about it in 1837. However, his system continued to be controversial at the institute and it was again banned. This second rejection did not dishearten the inventor: it drove him to develop his idea further.

As an accomplished cellist and organist, Braille had been appointed in 1834 to the position of organist in the Church of Saint-Nicolas-des-Champs and later at the Church of Saint-Vincent-de-Paul. This position required Braille to read musical scores, so he cleverly developed a six-dot system to represent musical notation. He then extended his idea by creating mathematical symbols to assist with his teaching of algebra and geometry. Yet, despite this continuous proof of the soundness and effectiveness of his system, it was still viewed with suspicion and was not adopted in the school.

At the age of 40, owing to a persistent respiratory illness, Louis was forced to leave his teaching post and move back to Coupvray. He had worked hard to convince a critical and blinkered audience that his system was both brilliant and effective, but it was – tragically – never nationally recognised in his lifetime.

Two days after his 43rd birthday, Louis Braille died. Then, only two years after his death, the RIBY finally acknowledged the legitimacy of Braille's method when the overwhelming insistence of his blind pupils forced them to do so.

In 1952, a hundred years after his death, Louis Braille's accomplishments were recognised by the French government and his body was exhumed from the village cemetery in his hometown of Coupvray and reburied in the Pantheon in Paris, with other French national heroes. However, as a gesture of final tribute, the Mayor of Coupvray insisted on having Braille's hands removed and reburied in the village cemetery as a final testament to his brilliance.

Braille's work changed the world of reading and writing for blind people, forever. Now, practically every country in the world uses books with braille; these books have double-sided pages to save space and this means that the books need not be so cumbersome. The Braille system has, importantly, helped blind people gain confidence and given them freedom to travel. And, the most vital point, blind people can now communicate independently, without needing print.

What a remarkable achievement! It is only marred by the fact that Braille himself never lived to see the widespread usage of his beloved invention.

Analyse the text

Table 8.1

Criteria	Examples from the text	
Paragraphs to organise ideas		
Cohesive devices within and across sentences and paragraphs (including adverbials)		
Selected verb forms for meaning and effect		
Co-ordinating and subordinating conjunctions	Co-ordinating	Subordinating
Wide range of clause structures in varying position (includes relative clauses) Subordinate clauses		
Capital letters/full stops		
Question marks		
Exclamation marks		
Apostrophes for possession		

Managing shifts between levels of formality through selecting vocabulary and manipulating grammatical structures Formal Informal			
Modal verbs			
Passive sentences			
Use of adverbs, preposition phrases and expanded noun phrases to add detail	**Adverbs**	**Preposition phrases**	**Expanded noun phrases**
Commas for lists			
Commas for clarity			
Punctuation for parenthesis including brackets and dashes (see also *Commas for clarity*)			
Semi-colons to mark the boundary between independent clauses			
Colons			
Hyphens			

Teacher's notes and ideas

Sentences can start with a co-ordinating conjunction such as 'and', 'but', 'or', 'yet', 'so'. These forms can be used for literary effect if used sparingly and intentionally. This needs explaining when analysing the text with the pupils.

You could compare the biography and autobiography texts on Louis Braille using the double bubble graphic organiser.

See the notes on Louis Braille's autobiography for further ideas.

Table 8.2

Criteria	Examples from the text	
Paragraphs to organise ideas	(As evidenced.)	
Cohesive devices within and across sentences and paragraphs (including adverbials)	...books were written in a Latin script that was raised above the page so that blind readers could follow the text by using their fingers: <u>this</u> was known as the Haüy system ('this' refers to the process described before the colon.) To begin with, Louis attended the local school... Louis stayed at <u>this</u> school for five years ('this' refers to the local school mentioned in the first sentence of the paragraph) Now, practically every country in the world uses books with braille; <u>these</u> books have double-sided pages to save space ('these books' refers to braille books.) <u>A</u> strong and continued belief in <u>his</u> invention inspired Braille to publish <u>another</u> book about <u>it</u> in 1837. (indefinite article 'a' + possessive adjective 'his' + determiner 'another' – refers back to a book already published by Braille + pronoun 'it' – refers back to musical and maths books written in braille in the previous paragraph.) It was a system that totally changed, <u>indeed</u> revolutionised, the lives of multitudes of blind people (The adverb 'indeed' accentuates the fact that braille changed people's lives.)	
Selected verb forms for meaning and effect	invented had been named living off use was to have was playing with	is used to punch being looked after continued to be had spread suffering could not learn	could follow was offered is means need not be
Co-ordinating and subordinating conjunctions	Co-ordinating	Subordinating
	and but so for neither ... nor yet	even though when where despite as while which after

Wide range of clause structure in varying position (includes relative clauses) Subordinate clauses	At the age of three, while his father was busy, Louis was playing with an awl (a sharp tool which is used to punch holes in leather) but it accidentally slipped, flew out of his hand and first pierced, then punctured, his left eye. Despite its popularity with the blind community, the teachers would not and could not see its validity. To begin with, Louis attended the local school, which unfortunately did not cater for pupils who were blind.
Capital letters/full stops	(As evidenced.)
Question marks	Why is he famous?
Exclamation marks	What a remarkable achievement!
Apostrophes for possession	Braille's father's Barbier's school's
Managing shifts between levels of formality through selecting vocabulary and manipulating grammatical structures Formal Informal	Louis Braille invented a tactile alphabet for the blind. It was a system that changed lives, enabling blind people of any age to read with the tips of their fingers. What a remarkable achievement! With great excitement, he spent hours, days and years simplifying and adapting a version of Barbier's idea. (This biography is formal and maintains this formality as is appropriate for this genre. There are only a few areas of informality evident here.)
Modal verbs	could, would, can
Passive sentences	…he was told… …this was known as the Haüy system, invented by Valentine Haüy …too complicated for the soldiers and therefore was neither developed nor used as a military tool …it was very quickly criticised and rejected, predominantly by sighted people. …he was forced to retire in 1840… …it was again banned… …it was still viewed with suspicion… …his body was exhumed from the village cemetery… …his eldest sibling had been named after his mother… …the second sibling, for some strange reason, had been given the same name as Louis… …Braille had been appointed in 1834 to the position of organist…

(continued)

Table 8.2 (*cont.*)

Use of adverbs, preposition phrases and expanded noun phrases to add detail	Adverbs	Preposition phrases	Expanded noun phrases

	totally
	simply
	accidentally
	tragically
	completely
	consequently
	miserably
	only
	extensively
	quickly
	perilously
	unfortunately
	easily
	quickly
	predominantly
	secretly
	only
	cleverly
	tragically
	finally
	importantly
	independently
	too
	now
	never
	today
	there
		in the village ceme-
		    tery
		    after his death
		at that time
		for blind people
		by creating
		    mathematical
		    symbols
		with his teaching of
		    algebra and
		    geometry
		at the age of three
			a tactile alphabet for
			    the blind
			a system that totally
			    changed, indeed
			    revolutionised, the
			    lives of multitudes
			    of blind people
			    by enabling them
			    to read
			the small town
			    of Coupvray in
			    France, just 20
			    miles east of Paris.
			his eldest sibling.
			a small, rural village
			    with many of its
			    inhabitants

Commas for lists	a small, rural village farmers used horses to plough their fields, for personal transporta- tion and for carrying heavy loads they use cars, tractors and trucks making harnesses, tack and saddles		

Commas for clarity	It was a system that totally changed, indeed revolutionised, the lives
	    of multitudes of blind people by enabling them to read, simply,
	    with the tips of their fingers…
	As a result, one of the most important jobs in the village was a lea-
	    ther worker; this was his father's profession.
	Louis had a happy childhood, spending many hours with his father
	    in his workshop playing with the multitude of tools but it was
	    there, in the workshop, that the unfortunate accident occurred
	    which was to have a massive impact on Louis for the rest of
	    his life.
	(Evidenced throughout the text.)		

Punctuation for parenthesis including brackets and dashes (see also *Commas for clarity*)	(Monique Catherine born 1793); (Louis-Simon born 1795); (born 1797) (a sharp tool which is used to punch holes in leather) (RIBY); (night lights were dangerous and, perilously, revealed their positions to the enemy) At that time, farmers used horses to plough their fields, for personal transportation and for carrying heavy loads – unlike today where they use cars, tractors and trucks. Even worse news came when Louis found out that the infection had spread to his right eye – and that there was no hope of saving it. He had worked hard to convince a critical and blinkered audience that his system was both brilliant and effective, but it was – tragically – never nationally recognised in his lifetime.
Semi-colons to mark the boundary between independent clauses	He was the fourth child of Monique and Simon-René: his eldest sibling had been named after his mother (Monique Catherine born 1793); the second sibling, for some strange reason, had been given the same name as Louis (Louis-Simon born 1795); and the third, Marie Céline (born 1797), managed to acquire an individual name for herself. As a result, one of the most important jobs in the village was a leather worker; this was his father's profession. However, things improved when he won a scholarship to the Royal Institution for Blind Youth in Paris (RIBY); he was then just 10 years old. Now, practically every country in the world uses books with braille; these books have double-sided pages to save space and this means that the books need not be so cumbersome.
Colons	It was a system that totally changed, indeed revolutionised, the lives of multitudes of blind people by enabling them to read, simply, with the tips of their fingers: an outstanding achievement. He was the fourth child of Monique and Simon-René: his eldest sibling had been named after his mother (Monique Catherine born 1793); the second sibling, for some strange reason, had been given the same name as Louis (Louis-Simon born 1795); and the third, Marie Céline (born 1797), managed to acquire an individual name for herself. Reading was still very challenging for him and books were not plentiful: the library only contained 14 huge books with raised letters, which made for very hard and slow reading. These books were written in a Latin script that was raised above the page so that blind readers could follow the text by using their fingers: this was known as the Haüy system, invented by Valentine Haüy (the founder of the RIBY).

(continued)

Table 8.2 (*cont.*)

	This system was slow, and Louis was impatient: he wanted to read quickly and he wanted to read extensively. This second rejection did not dishearten the inventor: it drove him to develop his idea further.	
Hyphens	Simon-René Louis-Simon top-secret	12-dot system first-ever double-sided

9　Autobiography of Louis Braille

Initially, this story was written in braille with my trusted friend, Alexandre François-René Pignier, translating it into Latin script so that more people can access it and read about my adventures. It is very hard, as a blind person, to know whom to trust to rewrite my story as I have to rely on their honesty and trustworthiness, but here goes!

I was born on 4 January 1809 in a small village called Coupvray 20 miles from Paris; it could take up to a day on horseback to reach Paris. My father would sometimes travel into Paris to sell some of his leather goods and occasionally stay away for at least a week; we would miss him and his warm, loving nature. Even though he worked hard, he still managed to spend time with each of his four children, either helping us read or showing us how to make harnesses, saddles and tack. In his spare time, he would play games with us – when there would be endless noise and laughter! We loved him very much.

My mother was loving too, in her own way. Her day started at dawn and was never finished until she went to bed: collecting water, baking bread, lighting the fire, cleaning, washing, helping in the fields, cooking, mending clothes and so on. She had no spare time so we didn't really get to know her well. Looking back on everything she did, I realise now that she showed her love by caring for us so conscientiously: for that I love her deeply.

Coupvray was very beautiful and I spent my very early childhood playing in the local woods and fields with my older brother and sisters. It was the memory of these times that would keep me going in my darker days. I'm not sure that I can recall the woods and fields properly now, but that doesn't matter, because what I do remember is the wondrous golden light that used to bounce off the trees in the morning. It always gave me hope.

That golden light was to be taken away from me at a very young age. I was never going to experience seeing my friends' faces light up when something good had happened nor see my siblings as adults. It all happened when I was three years old. At that age, my father would allow us to play in his workshop but one day he had been under a lot of pressure to finish a particular piece of work. While he was otherwise occupied, I grabbed an awl to punch holes in my scrap piece of leather, when it suddenly slipped, flew out of my hand and pierced my left eye. The agony was immense and my scream brought my father immediately to my side. However, the damage was done: forever.

I really don't remember very much over the next couple of months because the pain was so excruciating that I kept slipping between consciousness and unconsciousness. I vaguely remember a doctor in a long, black, woollen coat leaning over me with a very serious face, but the picture was very blurred.

The pain continued when, worse still, the infection travelled to my right eye. Eventually, by the age of five, the light went out completely and I found myself totally blind. My parents were distraught and joy did not enter our home again for many years. My father never forgave himself and this caused him to withdraw from the family: I never heard him laugh again and this was always a cause of great unhappiness for me.

At that time, I studied at the local school for five years but it was always very challenging as they didn't cater for students like myself. Luckily, I loved studying so I worked hard and through diligence I won a scholarship to the Royal Institute for Blind Youth in Paris (RIBY). Even though my parents were sad that I was to leave home at such a young age, they were relieved that I had secured an appropriate education for myself. Looking back at my time in the RIBY, I realise that it wasn't a good education but at least I spent time with other blind children, who could really understand how I felt.

Reading was always frustrating. For a start, there were only 14 books in the library and they were all written using the Haüy system. Valentine Haüy (the founder of the RIBY) had devised a method which meant that texts were written in a Latin script that was raised above the page so readers could feel their way along the lines. As a result, the books were heavy and awkward to carry around. I was absolutely sure there must be a better method.

This better method came in the form of Captain Charles Barbier de la Serre from the French army. He had invented a 12-dot system, which he called 'night writing', as a military tool. He was motivated to devise this method because he lost many soldiers at night when they were forced to light up their lanterns so that they could read the incoming dispatches. This alerted the enemy to their position and, as a consequence, soldiers were shot or ambushed. To prevent further deaths, Barbier designed this dot/dash system which operated through touch, not sight. Unfortunately, the system was too complicated and soldiers, who were predominantly uneducated, could not use it. Barbier then decided to bring his system to the blind community in the belief that they would gain from it. Sadly, it was met with suspicion and cynicism by an ignorant community – but not by me!

I was inspired and could see that, with some adaptation and a lot of thought, it could be made to work. Therefore, at the age of 12, I embarked on a three-year project to produce a new reading system for the blind. Every day, after finishing my homework, I would sit late into the night and muse over possible solutions. I tried many different formulae, tested them on other blind students and eventually proffered a solution. My blind colleagues were totally persuaded but the school's teachers banned it without even exploring its validity. No matter what I did, they would not accept it; after all, in their eyes I was only a child: what did I know? This was very dispiriting but I was never going to give up. In fact, I then went on to develop my theory further.

My mother had always wanted me to take up a musical instrument so I learnt the piano, later the organ, and then the cello. For me to continue pursuing my passion I had to learn how to read music. So, I devised a braille system for musical notation and could therefore translate any music for the blind to access. This enabled me to continue playing the organ for the Church of Saint-Nicolas-des-Champs and then, later, for the Church of Saint-Vincent-de-Paul. I was very proud of this achievement.

Later, when I was a teacher of algebra and geometry at the RIBY, I developed my system further. The students found my method invaluable but unfortunately I had to teach it covertly as braille was not supposed to be used at the school!

I taught at the RIBY until I was 40 years old. I didn't want to leave but I was pressurised to do so by a persistent respiratory illness. I'm lying here, now, exhausted and in great pain, reflecting sadly on my short life and wondering why my system to read for the blind was not accepted. It saddens me greatly that my invention was not seen to be good enough. I've had to fight against prejudice and ignorance within the sighted community and, unfortunately, I wasn't strong enough to win the battle. Now I am also losing the battle with my health and have no idea how much longer I will live.

It is 1852 and I've spent 38 years in darkness. I've learnt to live by seeing in my heart and soul. I see through people's words and the wind against my face but yet I have missed out, entirely, on colour and light. The days seem to stretch out endlessly and making an effort to try to do anything leaves me exhausted. There are no books to read unless someone reads to me. There is no organ for me to play nor countryside to appreciate. I am nearly bereft.

My parents died many years ago, as did my two sisters, Monique and Marie: they both died of consumption at a very young age. My brother, Louis-Simon, lost a leg in the war and now lives in poverty somewhere in Paris – I haven't seen him for many years. I know that I will perish soon leaving no legacy and that I will die in obscurity. I'm not sure who will want to read my ramblings but what else is there for me to do?

Louis Braille died on 6th January 1852, two days after his 43rd birthday. He would never see his invention gaining national and international acclaim. He would never know that his invention would change lives both then, and now, and he would never know that his name would become synonymous with his system of writing. Millions of people are hugely indebted to him: his legacy is truly remarkable.

Two years after his death a movement of blind students emerged to demand that the braille system be implemented. Following this pressure, relevant books were published in braille and the method has continued to this day. This allows people unfortunate enough to either be born blind, or who become blind for whatever reason, access to the real world by being able to read relatively easily – something people with normal sight have always taken for granted.

Braille was an unintended hero for blind people and as a result his name will live on into eternity.

Analyse the text

Table 9.1

Criteria	Examples from the text	
Paragraphs to organise ideas		
Cohesive devices within and across sentences and paragraphs (including adverbials, determiners, conjunctions, pronouns and ellipses)		
Selected verb forms for meaning and effect		
Co-ordinating and subordinating conjunctions	**Co-ordinating**	**Subordinating**
Wide range of clause structures in varying position Subordinate clauses		
Capital letters/full stops		
Question marks		
Apostrophes for contraction		
Managing shifts between levels of formality through selecting vocabulary and manipulating grammatical structures Formal Informal		

Modal verbs			
Passive sentences			
Use of adverbs, preposition phrases and expanded noun phrases to add detail	Adverbs	Preposition phrases	Expanded noun phrases
Commas for lists			
Commas for clarity			
Punctuation for parenthesis			
Semi-colons to mark the boundary between independent clauses			
Dashes			
Colons			
Hyphens			

Teacher's notes and ideas for the biography and autobiography of Louis Braille

Sentences can start with a co-ordinating conjunction such as 'and', 'but', 'or', 'yet', 'so'. These forms can be used for literary effect if used sparingly and intentionally. This needs explaining when analysing the text with the pupils.

The idea of having a biography and autobiography of the same person was to enable you to compare the differences. For example, an autobiography is a window into the writer's thoughts and feelings: it can be more informal and emotive but can have formal elements to it.

There are very few short autobiographies which have been written using the National Curriculum standards. Most autobiographies are in book form. However, you can use chapters of an autobiographical book to convert to a biography or write an autobiography from the perspective of another character. One great book to use is *Boy* by Roald Dahl.

Other activities you could explore are:

1   Learn how to read/write braille.
2   Find where braille is used nowadays (see the back of over-the-counter medication).
3   Ask someone from the RNIB (Royal National Institute of Blind People) to come in and talk about the charity.
4   Look at how dogs can be the eyes of a blind person. How else are dogs used for people with disabilities?
5   How would it change pupils' lives if they were blind?
6   Pupils could work in pairs (A is the blind person and B is the seer). B describes a picture/painting/situation for A to draw or guides them around a room with obstacles. How does it feel to be dependent on other people for vision?
7   Make a comparison with the loss of hearing.
8   Pupils write a poem to say what they will never see again if they suddenly become blind. This could be very emotional but the best poems come when pupils feel the depth of the emotion.
9   Look at why people write an autobiography. What is their legacy?
10   Louis Braille never gave up; he continued to believe that his method was the best one despite people's opinion. This is a good chance to teach resilience and how important it is to believe in yourself, not allowing other people to limit your abilities.

Table 9.2

Criteria	Examples from the text
Paragraphs to organise ideas	(As evidenced.)
Cohesive devices within and across sentences and paragraphs (including adverbials, determiners, conjunctions, pronouns and ellipses)	Pronouns – He/she/it/they/we/us My father never forgave himself and <u>this</u> caused him to withdraw ('<u>this</u>' refers back to his lack of forgiveness.) I was inspired and could see <u>that</u>, with some adaptation and a lot of thought, it could be made to work. It was the memory of <u>these</u> times <u>that</u> would keep me going in my darker days. ('<u>These</u> times' refers back to his childhood.) This better method… ('<u>this</u>' refers back to the previous paragraph.) …his invention (possessive adjective) …in her own way (refers to 'my mother'.) From this pressure… (relates back to the previous sentence.) (See section on adverbs and conjunctions for further evidence.)

Selected verb forms for meaning and effect	was written		was done
	access		kept slipping
	have to rely on		loved studying
	was born		had devised
	could take		were written
	worked		was motivated to devise
	helping/showing		didn't want to leave
	would keep me going		I've had to fight
Co-ordinating and subordinating conjunctions	**Co-ordinating**		**Subordinating**
	and		even though
	but		when
	so		because
	for		as
	but yet		which
			that
			until
			unless
Wide range of clause structures in varying position Subordinate clauses	Even though my parents were sad that I was to leave home at such a young age, they were relieved that I had secured an appropriate education for myself. Looking back at my time in the RIBY, I realise that it wasn't a good education but at least I spent time with other blind children, who could really understand how I felt. There are no books to read unless someone reads to me. In his spare time, he would play games with us – when there would be endless noise and laughter! (Not all clause structures are included.)		
Capital letters/full stops	(As evidenced.)		
Question marks	…what did I know? I'm not sure who will want to read my ramblings but what else is there for me to do?		
Apostrophes for contraction	I'm, doesn't, don't, didn't, wasn't, I've, haven't		
Managing shifts between levels of formality through selecting vocabulary and manipulating grammatical structures Formal Informal	I was born on 4 January 1809 in a small village called Coupvray 20 miles from Paris; it could take up to a day on horseback to reach Paris. My father would sometimes travel into Paris to sell some of his leather goods and occasionally stay away for at least a week; we would miss him and his warm, loving nature. Even though he worked hard, he still managed to spend time with each of his four children, either helping us read or showing us how to make harnesses, saddles and tack. In his spare time, he would play games with us – when there would be endless noise and laughter! We loved him very much.		

(*continued*)

Table 9.2 (*cont.*)

	My parents died many years ago, as did my two sisters, Monique and Marie: they both died of consumption at a very young age. My brother, Louis-Simon, lost a leg in the war and now lives in poverty somewhere in Paris – I haven't seen him for many years. I know that I will perish soon leaving no legacy and that I will die in obscurity. I'm not sure who will want to read my ramblings but what else is there for me to do? (First person) (Moves to a more formal third person recount.) Louis Braille died on 6th January 1852, two days after his 43rd birthday. He would never see his invention gaining national and international acclaim. He would never know that his invention would change lives both then, and now, and he would never know that his name would become synonymous with his system of writing. Millions of people are hugely indebted to him: his legacy is truly remarkable. (Text moves from the formality of factual information to the reader having access to how the writer feels throughout the text.)
Modal verbs	could, would, can, will, must
Passive sentences	…this story was written in braille. That golden light was to be taken away from me at a very young age. Sadly, it was met with suspicion and cynicism by an ignorant community… I had to teach it covertly as braille was not supposed to be used at the school! …the picture was very blurred. I was inspired… I was pressurised to do so by a persistent respiratory illness. …he had been under a lot of pressure to finish a particular piece of work.

Use of adverbs, pre-position phrases and expanded noun phrases to add detail	Adverbs	Preposition phrases	Expanded noun phrases
	initially occasionally really conscientiously early deeply properly suddenly immediately vaguely eventually completely totally luckily (Not all adverbs are included.)	with my trusted friend into Latin script in a small village called Coupvray 20 miles from Paris up to a day on horseback to reach Paris in her own way in the local woods and fields with my older brother and sisters (Not all preposition phrases are included.)	his leather goods his warm, loving nature each of his four children my very early childhood playing in the local woods the memory of these times the wondrous golden light that used to bounce off the trees in the morning a particular piece of work an awl to punch holes in my scrap piece of leather a cause of great unhappiness (Not all noun phrases are included.)

Commas for lists	...how to make harnesses, saddles and tack. ...collecting water, baking bread, lighting the fire, cleaning, washing, helping in the fields, cooking, mending clothes and so on.
Commas for clarity	Initially, this story was written in braille with my trusted friend, Alexandre François-René Pignier, translating it into Latin script so that more people can access it and read about my adventures. My mother was loving too, in her own way. I'm not sure that I can recall the woods and fields properly now, but that doesn't matter, because what I do remember is the wondrous golden light that used to bounce off the trees in the morning. At that age, my father would allow us to play in his workshop but one day he had been under a lot of pressure to finish a particular piece of work. He had invented a 12-dot system, which he called 'night writing', as a military tool. Unfortunately, the system was too complicated and soldiers, who were pre-dominantly uneducated, could not use it. My mother had always wanted me to take up a musical instrument so I learnt the piano, later the organ, and then the cello.
Punctuation for parenthesis	See also *Commas for clarity and dashes*. Valentine Haüy (the founder of the RIBY) had devised a method...
Semi-colons to mark the boundary between independent clauses	I was born on 4 January 1809 in a small village called Coupvray 20 miles from Paris; it could take up to a day on horseback to reach Paris. My father would sometimes travel into Paris to sell some of his leather goods and occasionally stay away for at least a week; we would miss him and his warm, loving nature. No matter what I did, they would not accept it; after all, in their eyes I was only a child: what did I know?
Dashes	In his spare time, he would play games with us – when there would be endless noise and laughter! Allowing people unfortunate enough to either be born blind or become blind for whatever reason, access to the real world by being able to read relatively easily – something people with normal sight have always taken for granted.
Colons	My mother was loving too, in her own way. Her day started at dawn and was never finished until she went to bed: collecting water, baking bread, lighting the fire, cleaning, washing, helping in the fields, cooking, mending clothes and so on. Looking back on everything she did, I realise now that she showed her love by caring for us so conscientiously: for that I love her deeply. However, the damage was done: forever.

(*continued*)

Table 9.2 (*cont.*)

	My father never forgave himself and this caused him to withdraw from the family: I never heard him laugh again and this was always a cause of great unhappiness for me. No matter what I did, they would not accept it; after all, in their eyes I was only a child: what did I know? My parents died many years ago, as did my two sisters, Monique and Marie: they both died of consumption at a very young age. Millions of people are hugely indebted to him: his legacy is truly remarkable.
Hyphens	François-René 12-dot three-year Saint-Nicolas-des-Champs Saint-Vincent-de-Paul Louis-Simon

10 Vikings Plunder Unsuspecting Monastery

Last month, Lindisfarne Monastery was raided and burnt to the ground by savage Vikings seeking treasure, food and lands.

The cold-hearted Vikings had departed from Scandinavia (Norway, Sweden and Denmark) to travel across the North Sea to the British Isles. They left their home country to move away from over-population, to seek adventure in new lands and to find greater wealth abroad. Taking to the seas in their longships, the Vikings showed their bravery by sailing and rowing across the rough and angry waters.

Their first landing place was the small island of Lindisfarne, also known as Holy Island, in the north of England.

The longships were made of green oak for the keel and rudder, wool and cotton for the red and white sails: they used metal nails to hold everything together. Finished off with terrifying dragons mounted on the prows of their ships, they looked like fierce dragons rearing up from the ocean floor, ready to kill anyone who tried to stop them in their murderous rampage.

Thirty men rowed 200 warriors across the North Sea to attack the peace-loving monks. Because their hulls were shallow, their craft could easily slide up onto the beaches allowing the brutal Vikings to surprise the praying monks. Alfred, who witnessed the event, said: 'The ships simply just glided onto the beach. The men from the seas then raced up to the monastery and fell upon the monks. The monks were powerless, terrified and easily overcome. I feel dreadful but I couldn't warn them any earlier – it all happened so quickly.'

The raging Vikings raced from the shore with astonishing speed, up to the monastery to surprise the hapless monks. They slaughtered everyone they met with their ornate axes, sharp swords and knives that plunged deep into the fleeing monks' hearts: slicing off many heads. The monastery was burnt to the ground, leaving only a few sorry stones. Everyone was murdered, animals were taken and the monastery's great wealth was shared out among the warriors. This was an easy battle as the monks were defenceless. Sweyn Forkbeard roared with pleasure; he was heard to shout: 'So much gold and so easy to take it.'

This horrific event is likely to be just the start of many Viking raids as the invaders are continuing to plunder the east coast of the British Isles. Let's hope one day they either leave our shores to return home, or, could they learn to stay and become peaceful citizens… perhaps?

In the meantime, how much longer can our native population cope with these raids? Many Anglo-Saxons are now too frightened to live on the east coast; they are leaving their old homes and moving further inland – what sort of life is that?

But the real message many Britons would love to pass on to the Vikings is: leave our island alone! And don't come back!

Analyse the text

Table 10.1

Criteria	Examples from the text
Proper nouns	
Preposition phrases	
Expanded noun phrases	
Hyphenated words	
Parenthesis (dashes)	
Parenthesis (brackets)	
Parenthesis (commas)	
Sentence showing a list of three actions separated by a comma and a co-ordinating conjunction	
Wide range of clause structures in varying position (beginning, middle and end of a sentence) Subordinate clauses	

Sentences using co-ordinating conjunctions	
Commas for lists	
Colons in a sentence	
Colons (found just before a quote)	
Quote (quote to add authenticity – inverted commas)	
Question	

Statement		
Fact	Opinion	Exclamation

Teacher's notes and ideas

Sentences can start with a co-ordinating conjunction such as 'and', 'but', 'or', 'yet', 'so'. These forms can be used for literary effect if used sparingly and intentionally. This needs explaining when analysing the text with the pupils.

Other headings for the newspaper could be LINDISFARNE RAIDED BY SAVAGE VIKINGS! or DEVASTATION OF MONASTERY BY VIKINGS! Pupils could come up with some of their own.

Before teaching this, use the story of Alfred witnessing the raid (also included in this book).

Give the pupils plenty of pictures and diagrams to explain the different parts of the ship. It helps if they understand that the hull of the ship was shallow, allowing Viking boats to land on beaches.

A good website is the BBC website on Vikings videos: www.bbc.co.uk/education/topics/ztyr9j6/videos/1

Table 10.2

Criteria	Examples from the text	
Proper nouns	Sweyn Forkbeard	North Sea
	Vikings	Holy Island
	British Isles	Lindisfarne
	Scandinavia (Norway, Sweden and Denmark)	England
Preposition phrases	by savage Vikings by sailing and rowing across the rough and angry waters in the north of England with terrifying dragons mounted on the prows of their ships in their murderous rampage	
Expanded noun phrases	the ground by savage Vikings their home country to move away from overpopulation 200 warriors across the North Sea to attack the peace-loving monks this horrific event	
Hyphenated words	cold-hearted Anglo-Saxons peace-loving	
Parenthesis (dashes)	I feel dreadful, but I couldn't warn them any earlier – it all happened so quickly. Many Anglo-Saxons are now too frightened to live on the east coast; they are leaving their old homes and moving further inland – what sort of life is that?	
Parenthesis (brackets)	...Scandinavia (Norway, Sweden and Denmark)...	
Parenthesis (commas)	Their first landing place was the small island of Lindisfarne, also known as Holy Island, in the north of England.	
Sentence showing a list of three actions separated by a comma and a co-ordinating conjunction	They left their home country to move away from overpopulation, to seek adventure in new lands and to find greater wealth abroad. Everyone was murdered, animals were taken and the monastery's great wealth was shared out among the warriors.	

Wide range of clause structures in varying position (beginning, middle and end of a sentence) Subordinate clauses	Taking to the seas in their longships, the Vikings showed their bravery by sailing and rowing across the rough and angry waters. Because their hulls were shallow, their craft could easily slide up onto the beaches allowing the brutal Vikings to surprise the praying monks. This was an easy battle as the monks were defenceless. This horrific event is likely to be just the start of many Viking raids as the invaders are continuing to plunder the east coast of the British Isles. Alfred, who witnessed the event, said:
Sentences using co-ordinating conjunctions	The men from the seas then raced up to the monastery <u>and</u> fell upon the monks. I feel dreadful <u>but</u> I couldn't warn them any earlier
Commas for lists	…by savage Vikings seeking treasure, food and lands. The longships were made of green oak for the keel and rudder, wool and cotton for the red and white sails: they used metal nails to hold everything together. They slaughtered everyone they met with their ornate axes, sharp swords and knives that plunged deep into the fleeing monks' hearts…
Colons in a sentence	The long ships were made of green oak for the keel and rudder, wool and cotton for the red and white sails: they used metal nails to hold everything together. They slaughtered everyone they met with their ornate axes, sharp swords and knives that plunged deep into the fleeing monks' hearts: slicing off many heads. But the real message many Britons would love to pass on to the Vikings is: leave our island alone! And don't come back!
Colons (found just before a quote)	Alfred, who witnessed the event, said: 'The ships simply just glided onto the beach…' Sweyn Forkbeard roared with pleasure; he was heard to shout: 'So much gold and so easy to take it.'
Quote (quote to add authenticity – inverted commas)	'The ships simply just glided onto the beach. The men from the seas then raced up to the monastery and fell upon the monks. The monks were powerless, terrified and easily overcome. I feel dreadful but I couldn't warn them any earlier – it all happened so quickly.' 'So much gold and so easy to take it.'
Question	Let's hope one day they either leave our shores to return home, or, could they learn to stay and become peaceful citizens… perhaps? In the meantime, how much longer can our native population cope with these raids? …what sort of life is that?

(continued)

Table 10.2 (*cont.*)

Statement		
Fact	Opinion	Exclamation
Lindisfarne Monastery was raided and burnt to the ground… Vikings had departed from Scandinavia (Norway, Sweden and Denmark) to travel across the North Sea to the British Isles. Their first landing place was the small island of Lindisfarne, also known as Holy Island, in the north of England. The longships were made of green oak for the keel and rudder, wool and cotton for the red and white sails and metal nails to hold it all together.	The cold-hearted Vikings… …the Vikings showed their bravery by sailing and rowing across the rough and angry waters… Finished off with a terrifying dragon… Finished off with <u>terrifying</u> drag-ons mounted on the prows of their ships, <u>they looked like fierce</u> <u>dragons rearing up from the ocean floor</u>…	But the real message many Britons would love to pass on to the Vikings is: leave our island alone! And don't come back!

11   The Dunkirk Miracle

Early on 26th May 1940, trapped by the might of the German army, our fearless soldiers were rescued from the beaches of Dunkirk by 800 small, civilian boats.

For four days, 330,000 soldiers, from the British Expeditionary Force (BEF) and the French army, had been stranded on the beaches of Dunkirk after trying, valiantly, to defend Belgium, Holland and France.

Unfortunately, the German army proved too powerful an enemy to hold back. The well-equipped Panzers were unstoppable, driving through and bombing anything, everything and anybody blocking their way.

There was fear in the hearts of the men who waited patiently for the boats to appear over the horizon: the boats intent on saving them. By some miracle, the 800 small boats had managed to make their way over the Channel; avoiding sea mines, the merciless Luftwaffe and the relentless shots being fired from the Dunkirk harbour, in their desperate attempt to ferry the waiting men from the beaches to the larger ships. Sergeant Reginald King said: 'After waiting and waiting for a boat to pick us up, one eventually turned up – and weren't we just over the moon!'

Conditions in the boats were horrendous, yet no one complained; the morale was high. Sergeant King went on to describe the perilous situation: 'We were stacked like sardines – one on top of the other – as they crammed as many men in as possible. The journey took four hours and the boat rolled and dipped and swerved – this way and then that way; some of the men were being sick, the others held the nausea back and, all of them – every single man – hung on, for his very life.'

Although many men were rescued, not everyone was as lucky. Some died attempting to reach a waiting boat; others were killed when the ship they were on was sunk. No one was out of danger until they had placed their feet on the welcoming shores of Britain, their homeland.

The amazing act of bravery, performed by hundreds of little boat owners, will show Hitler that the British will fight this war to its bitter conclusion and that our remarkable country will only end the war when it has freed all the occupied countries and vanquished their enemy. We should be proud of our boys and welcome them home, as heroes of the highest order.

Analyse the text

Table 11.1

Criteria	Examples from the text	
Describe setting and character to create atmosphere		
Cohesive devices within and across sentences and paragraphs (including adverbials, determiners, conjunctions, pronouns and ellipses)		
Verb forms		
Conjunctions	**Co-ordinating**	**Subordinating**
Exclamation marks		
Commas for lists		
Passive sentences		
Modal verbs		
Inverted commas		
Wide range of clause structures in varying position		
Subordinate clauses		

Use of adverbs, preposition phrases and expanded noun phrases to add detail	Adverbs	Preposition phrases	Expanded noun phrases
Commas for clarity			
Punctuation for parenthesis (dashes) See *Commas for clarity* for further punctuation			
Semi-colons to mark the boundary between independent clauses			
Colons			
Hyphens			
Managing shift between levels of formality			
Alternative headlines			
Fact or opinion	Fact		Opinion

Teacher's notes and ideas

This can be taught in conjunction with the letter home from the Dunkirk beaches. There are many YouTube videos and a considerable amount of information online explaining what happened. This pre-work will really support the understanding of the context.

This is a comparative text to the letter home, also found in this book, as it is more formal and less emotional. It is about being upbeat and celebrating the success to instil morale. Many of the soldiers believed that they would be decried for failing and having to retreat but instead they were welcomed home and highly praised.

It would be good to explore whether the same thing could happen now. Would civilians be asked to risk life and boat to save soldiers?

To introduce the topic, give the pupils a series of pictures, maps, videos and audio recordings for them to work out why the soldiers were on the Dunkirk beach.

You could look at bias as well as fact and opinion and how a fact can be interlaced with an opinion: opinions usually come in the form of an adjective or adverb to add more detail.

Table 11.2

Criteria	Examples from the text
Describe setting and character to create atmosphere	By some miracle, the 800 small boats had managed to make their way over the Channel; avoiding sea mines, the merciless Luftwaffe and the relentless shots being fired from the Dunkirk harbour, in their desperate attempt to ferry the waiting men from the beaches to the larger ships. Conditions in the boats were horrendous, yet no one complained; the morale was high. Sergeant King went on to describe the perilous situation: 'We were stacked like sardines – one on top of the other – as they crammed as many men in as possible. The journey took four hours and the boat rolled and dipped and swerved – this way and then that way; some of the men were being sick, the others held the nausea back and, all of them – every single man – hung on, for his very life.'
Cohesive devices within and across sentences and paragraphs (including adverbials, determiners, conjunctions, pronouns and ellipses)	…this way and that way – (Expands on the previous words 'rolled, dipped and swerved'.) After waiting and waiting for a boat to pick us up, <u>one</u> eventually turned up ('one' relates back to the 'boat'.) …will show Hitler that the British will fight <u>this</u> war to its bitter conclusion – (Demonstrative 'this' to refer back to the whole event and why the men were stranded in Dunkirk.) …soldiers, from the British Expeditionary Force…stranded on the beaches of Dunkirk after trying…to defend Belgium, Holland and France. <u>Unfortunately</u>, the German army proved too powerful an enemy to hold back. ('unfortunately' leads the reader to the reason for the men being on the beaches after failing to defend Europe.) <u>No one</u> was out of danger until <u>they</u> had placed <u>their</u> feet on the welcoming shores of Britain, <u>their</u> homeland. (The pronouns 'they' and 'no one' and possessive adjective 'their' relate to the stranded soldiers.)

Verb forms	trapped were rescued had been stranded to defend driving was had managed to make being fired	were rolled and dipped and swerved were being sick were rescued had placed will fight has freed should be
Co-ordinating and subordinating conjunctions	**Co-ordinating**	**Subordinating**
	and yet for	when although after as until
Exclamation marks	'…and weren't we just over the moon!'	
Commas for lists	Belgium, Holland and France. …avoiding sea mines, the merciless Luftwaffe and the relentless shots being fired from the Dunkirk harbour… …anything, everything and anybody blocking their way.	
Passive sentences	…330,000 soldiers, from the British Expeditionary Force (BEF) and the French army, had been stranded on the beaches of Dunkirk…	
Modal verbs	will, should	
Inverted commas	Sergeant Reginald King said: 'After waiting and waiting for a boat to pick us up, one eventually turned up – and weren't we just over the moon!' Sergeant King went on to describe the perilous situation: 'We were stacked like sardines – one on top of the other – as they crammed as many men in as possible. The journey took four hours and the boat rolled and dipped and swerved – this way and then that way; some of the men were being sick, the others held the nausea back and, all of them – every single man – hung on, for his very life.'	
Wide range of clause structures in varying position Subordinate clauses	Early on 26th May 1940, trapped by the might of the German army, our fearless soldiers were rescued from the beaches of Dunkirk by 800 small boats. Although many men were rescued, not everyone was as lucky. For four days, 330,000 soldiers, from the British Expeditionary Force (BEF) and the French army, had been stranded on the beaches of Dunkirk after trying, valiantly, to defend Belgium, Holland and France. No one was out of danger until they had placed their feet on the welcoming shores of Britain, their homeland. After waiting and waiting for a boat to pick us up, one eventually turned up – and weren't we just over the moon!	

(continued)

Table 11.2 (*cont.*)

Use of adverbs, preposition phrases and expanded noun phrases to add detail	Adverbs	Preposition phrases	Expanded noun phrases
	valiantly unfortunately patiently eventually only too	for four days early on 26th May 1940 by some miracle from the British Expeditionary Force (BEF) and the French army on the beaches of Dunkirk	the might of the German army our fearless soldiers the well-equipped Panzers fear in the hearts of the men who waited patiently for the boats to appear over the horizon 800 little boats their desperate attempt to ferry the waiting men stacked like sardines – one on top of the other the amazing act of bravery
Commas for clarity	For four days, 330,000 soldiers, from the British Expeditionary Force (BEF) and the French army, had been stranded on the beaches of Dunkirk after trying, valiantly, to defend Belgium, Holland and France. By some miracle, the 800 small boats had managed to make their way over the Channel… The journey took four hours and the boat rolled and dipped and swerved – this way and then that way; some of the men were being sick, the others held the nausea back and, all of them – every single man – hung on, for his very life.		
Punctuation for parenthesis (dashes) See *Commas for clarity* for further punctuation	We were stacked like sardines – one on top of the other – as they crammed as many men in as possible. The journey took four hours and the boat rolled and dipped and swerved – this way and then that way; some of the men were being sick, the others held the nausea back and, all of them – every single man – hung on, for his very life.		
Semi-colons to mark the boundary between independent clauses	By some miracle, the 800 small boats had managed to make their way over the Channel; avoiding sea mines, the merciless Luftwaffe and the relentless shots being fired from the Dunkirk harbour, in their desperate attempt to ferry the waiting men from the beaches to the larger ships. Conditions in the boats were horrendous, yet no one complained; the morale was high. The journey took four hours and the boat rolled and dipped and swerved – this way and then that way; some of the men were being sick, the others held the nausea back and, all of them – every single man – hung on, for his very life. Some died attempting to reach a waiting boat; others were killed when the ship they were on was sunk.		

Colons	There was fear in the hearts of the men who waited patiently for the boats to appear over the horizon: the boats intent on saving them. Sergeant Reginald King said: 'After waiting and waiting for a boat to pick us up, one eventually turned up – and weren't we just over the moon!' Conditions in the boats were horrendous, yet no one complained; the morale was high. Sergeant King went on to describe the perilous situation: 'We were stacked like sardines – one on top of the other – as they crammed as many men in as possible.'
Hyphens	well-equipped
Managing shift between levels of formality	For four days, 330,000 soldiers, from the British Expeditionary Force (BEF) and the French army, had been stranded on the beaches of Dunkirk after trying, valiantly, to defend Belgium, Holland and France. (Starts very factually.) There was fear in the hearts of the men who waited patiently for the boats to appear over the horizon: the boats intent on saving them. (Becomes more emotive.) Conditions in the boats were horrendous, yet no one complained; the morale was high. Sergeant King went on to describe the perilous situation: (Jumps in and out of factual to emotive.) '…and weren't we just over the moon!' (Informal speech) The amazing act of bravery, performed by hundreds of little boat owners, will show Hitler that the British will fight this war to its bitter conclusion and that our remarkable country will only end the war when it has freed all the occupied countries and vanquished their enemy. (Finishes with an uplifting and determined approach to the war.)
Alternative headlines	Dunkirk defence defies German forces Tens of thousands safely home Hundreds of small boats save our brave men

Fact or opinion	Fact	Opinion
	…trapped by the might of the German army, our fearless soldiers were rescued from the beaches of Dunkirk by 800 small, civilian boats. For four days, 330,000 soldiers, from the British Expeditionary Force (BEF) and the French army, had been stranded on the beaches of Dunkirk… The well-equipped Panzers were unstoppable… 800 small boats had managed to make their way over the Channel… The journey took four hours… Although many men were rescued, not everyone was as lucky…	There was fear in the hearts of the men who waited patiently…(How do we know that all the men had fear in their hearts? – some of them might have been too exhausted to care, others might have been relieved.) …trying, valiantly, to defend Belgium, Holland and France.

(continued)

Table 11.2 (*cont.*)

	No one was out of danger until they had placed their feet on the welcoming shores of Britain…	soldiers (How do we know that they <u>all</u> fought valiantly?) <u>By some miracle</u> the merciless Luftwaffe (Was it really a miracle or should we put it down to hard work and skill?) Conditions in the boats were <u>horrendous</u>… (Were all the conditions on all 800 boats horrendous?) The amazing act of bravery… (Some people saw it as an act of bravery while others viewed it as a necessity to help rescue the soldiers.) We should be proud of our boys… ('Should' is an obligation from someone's opinion.)

The above fact/opinion table is not definitive.

It isn't easy to divide between fact and opinion because some facts can be littered with opinion or generalisations such as 'some', 'all', 'everybody' or an adjective such as 'horrendous' (which is an opinion). For some of the soldiers, the journey home might not have been horrendous but news reports will sensationalise and generalise the event, putting forward the slant that best suits its purpose.

When the article says, 'Unfortunately, the German army proved too powerful an enemy to hold back', who is it unfortunate for? If a German was reading the paper, it would have been viewed as fortunate.

12   Letter Home from a Soldier

My darling wife and dearest family,

We set off from Britain, positive that we would win the war quickly and teach the Germans a lesson, but their might has been too much for us. They had obviously been preparing for this war long before we had even realised it was even a possibility. This has meant that hundreds of thousands of our good men are now dying here in Belgium, Holland and France.

I joined the British Expeditionary Force (BEF) at the beginning of the war because I thought it was the right thing to do, but I'm not so sure now – we should have listened to those who fought in World War I. We fought hard but were pushed back to the beaches of Dunkirk where we are now stranded. Bombs have rained down on us daily, threatening our very existence.

Waiting for something to happen is driving men mad. I have no idea what each day will bring with it, death or rescue? William, my sergeant and best friend, lies next to me fighting for his life: his leg has been blown half off and there is no hope of any medical help. He rambles on mentioning various names; I think they are his family but nothing he says seems to make any sense.

There is a constant noise of firing and bombs dropping from Luftwaffe planes onto the brave men who are trying to rescue us, but with so few ships and so many men to pick us up, it could take many days before I get on board one of them. The remorseless noise is keeping me awake at night and I just crave for silence: I think when I get home I will find the quietest space in Britain and live there forever!

As far as the eye can see, there are endless lines of men waiting patiently, fervently hoping that they'll get a chance to see their loved ones again. Despite the desperation of the situation, men are behaving as normally as possible: the band is playing on the bandstand, entertaining those who want to listen; horse races and betting is allowed so that men can spend their accumulated money and soldiers are fighting over card games. I can see large ships sitting out in the water hoping to fill up with exhausted soldiers and smaller boats, loaded with quiet men, ferrying back and forth from the shore. Some men are so desperate that they're attempting to swim the distance and, tragically, many have lost their lives by drowning. I'm scared that I won't be coming home, as hope and time are running out, but I'm gritting my teeth, and hoping, hoping...

I'm just thinking how much I miss everything about my life and my family. All I can do now is pray that I'll be given the chance to see you and my children again: God willing, God willing.

If I don't come home, look after each other and make sure you live your lives with purpose and love and, just know, know that I love you all.

Love you always

Fred

Analyse the text

Table 12.1

Criteria	Examples from the text	
Describe setting and character to create atmosphere		
Cohesive devices within and across sentences and paragraphs (including adverbials, determiners, conjunctions, pronouns and ellipses)		
Different verb forms (changes throughout the letter)		
Co-ordinating and subordinating conjunctions	Co-ordinating	Subordinating
Commas for lists		
Apostrophes for contraction		
Selecting vocabulary and grammatical structures		

Modal verbs			
Wide range of clause structures in varying position Subordinate clauses			
Use of adverbs, preposition phrases and expanded noun phrases to add detail	Adverbs	Preposition phrases	Expanded noun phrases
Commas for clarity			
Punctuation for parenthesis			
Question marks			
Exclamation marks			
Managing shifts between levels of formality			
Semi-colons to mark the boundary between independent clauses			
Dashes			
Colons			

Teacher's notes and ideas

This was a great unit of work which used some of the senses to write the letter. So when the pupils planned their letter, it was broken up into sections: what they saw, heard and felt. This was all done after watching the section of *Atonement* where they were awaiting rescue. (There is some swearing so play it with the sound off until the music starts. Watch it several times, allowing pupils a chance to assimilate many ideas.)

Get the pupils to act out some of the scenes. Some drama conventions can be found on the following website: http://dramaresource.com/drama-strategies/

This activity can be followed with, or preceded by, writing a newspaper article reporting on the Dunkirk evacuation (also included in the book).

The BBC History website includes a short animation demonstrating the big picture of why the soldiers ended up on the Dunkirk beaches (www.bbc.co.uk/history/worldwars/wwtwo/launch_ani_fall_france_campaign.shtml).

For background information, see www.iwm.org.uk/history/what-you-need-to-know-about-the-dunkirk-evacuations

Further activities could be:

1 Diary entry of a child in England waiting for her father to return. He could either have been a soldier in the BEF or one of the civilians that volunteered their services on one of the 800 small boats. You could start the story from when the family sat around the radio listening to the announcement. Play the announcement to the pupils: www.bbc.co.uk/archive/dunkirk/14312.shtml

2 Another piece of writing could be a flashback story. Start the story with an old lady looking at a photograph in the present day. She then retells the story, jumping back and forth from the past to the present. Different objects, short videos or music reignite an image or memory for her, in order for her to continue retelling the story. If you could access artefacts for the pupils to use, this would make it more realistic and powerful.

3 When a soldier joins the army, they have to write a letter home in the event of their death. You will find some examples on the following website: www.dailymail.co.uk/news/article-2094898/Heartbreaking-letters-frontline-soldiers-came-home-revealed.html. Pupils could write their own letters.

4 You can read letters to loved ones on the Imperial War Museum website: www.iwm.org.uk/history/letters-to-loved-ones

This is a very emotional piece of writing; it engages the boys and reluctant writers.

Structure of the letter

1 Why we set off
2 Regret
3 What is happening around me
4 What I can hear
5 What I can see and how it makes me feel
6 Looking to the future

Table 12.2

Criteria	Examples from the text	
Describe setting and character to create atmosphere	As far as the eye can see, there are endless lines of men waiting patiently, fervently hoping that they'll get a chance to see their loved ones again. Despite the desperation of the situation, men are behaving as normally as possible: the band is playing on the bandstand, entertaining those who want to listen; horse races and betting is allowed so that men can spend their accumulated money and soldiers are fighting over card games. I can see large ships sitting out in the water hoping to fill up with exhausted soldiers and smaller boats, loaded with quiet men, ferrying back and forth from the shore. Some men are so desperate that they're attempting to swim the distance and, tragically, many have lost their lives by drowning. I'm scared that I won't be coming home, as hope and time are running out, but I'm gritting my teeth, and hoping, hoping…	
Cohesive devices within and across sentences and paragraphs (including adverbials, determiners, conjunctions, pronouns and ellipses)	<u>This</u> has meant that <u>this</u> war so <u>that</u> men can spend their accumulated money we should have listened to <u>those</u> who fought in World War I <u>before</u> I get on board <u>one of them</u>. thousands of <u>our</u> good men are now dying here in Belgium tragically many have lost <u>their</u> lives by drowning each day brings with <u>it</u> death or rescue as hope and time are running out, but I'm gritting my teeth, and hoping, hoping… (For conjunctions and adverbials, see below)	
Different verb forms (changes throught the letter)	set off would teach has been had obviously been preparing had even realised joined I'm should have listened have rained down waiting	will bring lies rambles could take is keeping is allowed are fighting can see they're attempting to swim won't be coming
Co-ordinating and subordinating conjunctions	Co-ordinating	Subordinating
	and but so	before because when if
Commas for lists	Belgium, Holland and France	

(continued)

Table 12.2 (*cont.*)

Apostrophes for contraction	I'm　　　　　　　　won't they'll　　　　　　　I'll they're　　　　　　　don't		
Selecting vocabulary and grammatical structures	Jumps between past, present and future throughout the text. Informality punctuated with the formality of explaining the situation. First person – gives first-hand experience Final three paragraphs focus on what they felt, what they heard and what they saw. Emotional but factual		
Modal verbs	could, would, can, will, should		
Wide range of clause structures in varying position Subordinate clauses	There is a constant noise of firing and bombs dropping from Luftwaffe planes onto the brave men who are trying to rescue us, but with so few ships and so many men to pick us up, it could take many days before I get on board one of them. I joined the British Expeditionary Force (BEF) at the beginning of the war because I thought it was the right thing to do, but I'm not so sure now – we should have listened to those who fought in World War I. If I don't come home, look after each other and make sure you live your lives with purpose and love and, just know, know that I love you all.		
Use of adverbs, preposition phrases and expanded noun phrases to add detail	**Adverbs**	**Preposition phrases**	**Expanded noun phrases**
	as far as the eye can see quickly obviously daily patiently fervently normally tragically	in World War I on the bandstand with so few ships with exhausted soldiers despite the desperation of the situation	the beaches of Dunkirk the brave men who are trying to rescue us endless lines of men those who want to listen smaller boats, loaded with quiet men, those who want to listen their accumulated money

Commas for clarity	We set off from Britain, positive that we would win the war quickly and teach the Germans a lesson, but their might has been too much for us. Bombs have rained down on us daily, threatening our very existence. William, my sergeant and best friend, lies next to me fighting for his life: his leg has been blown half off and there is no hope of any medical help.
Punctuation for parenthesis	See *Commas for clarity*. I joined the British Expeditionary Force (BEF) at the beginning of the war because I thought it was the right thing to do, but I'm not so sure now – we should have listened to those who fought in World War I.
Question marks	I have no idea what each day will bring with it, death or rescue?
Exclamation marks	The remorseless noise is keeping me awake at night and I just crave for silence: I think when I get home I will find the quietest space in Britain and live there forever!
Managing shifts between levels of formality	Starts with informality when addressing his family – 'My darling wife and dearest family,' It then moves into a formal explanation of the situation – 'This has meant that hundreds of thousands of our good men are now dying…' Within paragraphs it moves from personal informal language – 'the right thing to do' – to explanations of the what had happened – 'We fought hard but were pushed back to the beaches of Dunkirk where we are now stranded.' The last line then uses figurative language to create a more poetical image – 'Bombs have rained down on us daily, threatening our very existence.'
Semi-colons to mark the boundary between independent clauses	He rambles on mentioning various names; I think they are his family but nothing he says seems to make any sense. Semi-colon in a list – 'Despite the desperation of the situation, men are behaving as normally as possible: the band is playing on the bandstand, entertaining those who want to listen; horse races and betting is allowed so that men can spend their accumulated money and soldiers are fighting over card games.'
Dashes	I joined the British Expeditionary Force (BEF) at the beginning of the war because I thought it was the right thing to do, but I'm not so sure now – we should have listened to those who fought in World War I.

(continued)

Table 12.2 (*cont.*)

Colons	Despite the desperation of the situation, men are behaving as normally as possible: the band is playing on the bandstand, entertaining those who want to listen; horse races and betting is allowed so that men can spend their accumulated money and soldiers are fighting over card games. William, my sergeant and best friend, lies next to me fighting for his life: his leg has been blown half off and there is no hope of any medical help. The remorseless noise is keeping me awake at night and I just crave for silence: I think when I get home I will find the quietest space in Britain and live there forever!

13   The Lifecycle of the Mayfly

Introduction

The mayfly is a medium-sized insect that is found in a variety of habitats all around the world. In the insect community it is most closely related to the dragonfly and damselfly. Worldwide there are at least 2,500 species of mayfly; in North America alone there are nearly 630 varieties. It is found, exclusively, in or on water and mainly in rivers, lakes or ponds.

It appears briefly in adult form but has a hugely important impact on its habitat.

The lifecycle

The mayfly's lifecycle sees the females flying directly into a swarm of males where they will mate in flight. The male will use its elongated legs to hook a female, preventing other males from mating with her. After the male releases the female, she falls to the surface of the water where she lays thousands of eggs. Once she has laid the eggs, she will not resume flight but lie on the surface where she will be incorporated into the pond or river food chain. The male will not return to water but die on the riverbank.

What happens to the eggs?

Some females will dive down to the bottom and attach the eggs to plants or stones to avoid them drifting off while others rely on the eggs to sink and self-attach.

This stage can take between a couple of days and two weeks before the eggs hatch into nymphs. These nymphs can then spend up to two years building up resources for the sub-imago and imago stages: this can however, depend on the species of mayfly and the conditions of the habitat. Despite many nymphs surrendering to prey, there are still many millions more that make adulthood.

From nymph to adult: nymph, sub-imago, imago

The nymphs emerge from their watery life to embark on a life on the wing. They will discard their nymphal shuck and transform into the sub-imago (the first stage of adulthood). Once emerged and free, the sub-imago will hide in the vegetation surrounding the pond or river to protect themselves from further predation. It is at this point that these newly formed creatures, which are drying their unremarkable wings, are defenseless and most likely to become a part of the food chain.

The stage only lasts a few hours before it emerges into the brightly coloured species we see hovering above the riverbanks - this is now an imago (the second adult stage).

The mayfly is unique because it has the ability to produce two entirely different winged adult forms in its lifecycle – remember that a butterfly has only one adult stage – and as an adult, it has one of the most short-lived lives in the animal kingdom. It can live from half an hour to 24 hours: not long. During the imago stage, the mayfly does not eat.

Why is the mayfly remarkable?

Many species emerge from the water and metamorphose at the same time. This event can cause many problems for some towns and cities. For example in Mississippi - North America - over 18 trillion insects hatch simultaneously. They are then attracted to nearby towns' lights where they die. This cause piles of rotting corpses that, if not removed, will create heath and odour issues. The vast piles of mayflies are removed by snow ploughs and buried.

Not all parts of the world view the swarm as an irritation. It is now becoming known that insects are protein-rich and offer a valuable food resource for those parts of the world where food is scarce. Inhabitants that live near Lake Victoria in Africa make a patty called 'Kungu' out of the adult mayfly: this supplements their poor diet.

Conclusion

This remarkable insect – yes it is remarkable – is a food source for thousands of different animals and is a vital part of the food chain. Without them many animals would die. As much as we see them as a nuisance, they are vital to many different habitats and so are essential to the delicate balance and harmony of nature. Their loss could have a serious impact on the human race.

Analyse the text

Table 13.1

Criteria	Examples from the text	
Paragraphs to organise ideas		
Cohesive devices within and across sentences and paragraphs (including adverbials, determiners, conjunctions, pronouns and ellipses)		
Different verb forms		
Questions		
Co-ordinating and subordinating conjunctions	Co-ordinating	Subordinating
Capital letters and full stops		
Vocabulary and grammatical structures reflect level of formality	Present tense: Technical vocabulary: Factual-based adjectives: Opinion vocabulary:	

(continued)

Table 13.1 (*cont.*)

Modal verbs			
Wide range of clause structures in varying position Subordinate clauses			
Use of adverbs, preposition phrases and expanded noun phrases to add detail	Adverbs	Prepositions	Expanded noun phrases
Commas for clarity			
Apostrophes for possession			
Hyphens			
Semi-colons to mark the boundary between independent clauses			
Colons			
Dashes			

Teacher's notes and ideas

1 This could be done after looking at the difference between the lifecycle of a butterfly and a mayfly. The pupils will understand the difference better.
2 There are video clips of the mayfly siege in Canada, where they used snow ploughs to clear up the dead insects. Some useful clips are:
www.youtube.com/watch?v=PBHBfck67D8
www.bbc.co.uk/nature/life/Mayfly
www.youtube.com/watch?v=1r1wxLKhE2o
www.youtube.com/watch?v=V0V1-0alTMY
3 The features lend themselves to other scientific information texts.
4 Pupils could draw the lifecycle from the text.

Table 13.2

Criteria	Examples from the text	
Paragraphs to organise ideas	(As evidenced.)	
Cohesive devices within and across sentences and paragraphs (including adverbials, determiners, conjunctions, pronouns and ellipses)	After the male releases the female, she falls to the surface of the water where she lays thousands of eggs. Once she has laid the eggs… (once refers back to the laying of the eggs) The mayfly is a medium-sized insect that is found in a variety of habitats all around the world. It appears briefly in adult form… ('It' refers to the mayfly from the previous paragraph.)	
Different verb forms	is is found appears will mate	will use will be incorporated to avoid see hovering
Questions	What is so incredible about the mayfly? What happens to the eggs? Why is the mayfly remarkable?	
Co-ordinating and subordinating conjunctions	Co-ordinating	Subordinating
	and but for	that where after once while despite which because if
Capital letters and full stops	(As evidenced.)	

(continued)

Table 13.2 (*cont.*)

Vocabulary and grammatical structures reflect level of formality	Present tense: is found, appears Technical vocabulary: sub-imago, lifecycle, swarm, nymphal shuck Factual based adjectives: medium-sized, variety, important, elongated Opinion vocabulary: remarkable, delicate, vast
Modal verbs	could, would, will, can
Wide range of clause structures in varying position Subordinate clauses	Once she has laid the eggs, she will not resume flight but lie on the surface where she will be incorporated into the pond or river food chain. Despite many nymphs surrendering to prey, there are still many millions more that make adulthood. This cause piles of rotting corpses that, if not removed, will create heath and odour issues. It is at this point that these newly formed creatures, which are drying their unremarkable wings, are defenseless and most likely to become a part of the food chain.

Use of adverbs, preposition phrases and expanded noun phrases to add detail	Adverbs	Prepositions	Expanded noun phrases
	nearly exclusively mainly hugely briefly directly newly likely only entirely simultaneously	around the world in the insect community after the male releases the female, up to two years during this adult stage	this remarkable insect a food source for thousands of different animals essential to the delicate balance and harmony of nature this supplements their poor diet piles of rotting corpses the animal kingdom two entirely different winged adult forms in its lifecycle

Commas for clarity	It is found, exclusively, in or on water and mainly in rivers, lakes or ponds. After the male releases the female, she falls to the surface of the water where she lays thousands of eggs. Once she has laid the eggs, she will not resume flight but lie on the surface where she will be incorporated into the pond or river food chain. These nymphs can then spend up to two years building up resources for the sub-imago and imago stages: this can however, depend on the species of mayfly and the conditions of the habitat.
Apostrophes for possession	A mayfly's lifecycle
Hyphens	medium-sized short-lived sub-imagos protein-rich

Semi-colons to mark the boundary between independent clauses	Worldwide there are at least 2,500 species of mayfly; in North America alone there are nearly 630 varieties.
Colons	These nymphs can then spend up to two years building up resources for the sub-imago and imago stages: this can however, depend on the species of mayfly and the conditions of the habitat. From nymph to adult: nymph, sub-imago, imago This stage only last a few hours before it emerges into the brightly coloured species we see hovering above the riverbanks - this is now an imago (their final stage): and this is the incredible part of the mayfly's lifecycle. It can live from half an hour to 24 hours: not long. Inhabitants that live near Lake Victoria in Africa make a patty called 'Kungu' out of the adult mayfly: this supplements their poor diet.
Dashes	This stage only last a few hours before it emerges into the brightly coloured species we see hovering above the riverbanks – this is now an imago (their final stage): For example in Mississippi – North America – over 18 trillion insects hatch simultaneously.

14 What Do You Cook a Fussy, Grumpy Dragon?

At one and the same time, cooking for a dragon can be a very dangerous but exciting event. However, before you even buy or prepare this particular dish, I strongly recommend you purchase fireproof gloves because many of the ingredients could seriously burn your hands.

If you are unlucky enough to know a bad-tempered dragon, then it might be better to exclude, or reduce, some of the hotter ingredients, which will make the dish less harmful to humans and other animals. However, if you are lucky enough to know a good-natured dragon, then you can be generous with the spicier elements of the recipe. Unfortunately, there are more bad-tempered dragons, who can be extremely grumpy if the dish is not hot enough. Be warned: the hotter you make the dish the more irritable the dragon will become.

The following equipment is needed, or rather, is essential:

- Fireproof gloves – preferably arm's length, but it would be all right if they only come up to the elbow.
- Fluorescent blue, bulletproof vest would be a good idea as sometimes the ingredients can be very volatile and behave like bullets from a machine gun; this has the potential to kill the chef.
- One steel and shatterproof glass helmet. I know this is a bit heavy but you're better protected than dead.

Now you are ready to mix your explosive ingredients. Preparation is essential or death will be a certainty.

Ingredients for cooking:

- The smoke of an underwater, active volcano collected during the night with a full moon.
- 400g of charcoal embers heated to exactly 51°C (don't let the temperature drop below 49°C).
- 50 red slugs, which have been feeding on red-hot chillies for over one month. (It is the chillies which give the dish its red colour.)
- 100 fire-eating ants from the Amazonian rainforest, preferably collected very early in the morning, as they are much spicier then.
- 200g of fat for basting.

Method, or rather how to bung them all together:

1 Cover half the slugs with the fat.
2 Heat half the slugs in the microwave for 3 minutes and put the other half with the fat in the oven for 15 minutes.
3 Danger: be careful as the microwave can cause the slugs to explode. You have been warned!
4 Take the slugs out of the oven and microwave and place them in the smoke of the active volcano. This gives it a great smoky flavour.

5 Mix in the live fire-eating ants. This can be a bit tricky because they try to escape. Once they've escaped they can be very angry and sting anything or anyone in sight.

6 Sprinkle the charcoal embers on top, just to add flavour.

This recipe has proved successful in the past but many people have not survived the ordeal. All I can say is good luck. You will need it!

Analyse the text

Table 14.1

Criteria	Examples from the text
Fronted adverbials	
Preposition phrases	
Formal language	
Subordinating conjunctions / subordinate clauses	
Relative clauses	
Exclamation mark	
Dash	
Hyphenated words	
Co-ordinating conjunctions / co-ordinate clauses	

Question	
Colons	
Commas to separate lists	
Apostrophes for contraction	
Conditional verbs	
Semi-colons in a sentence	
Swapping from formal to informal language	
Variety of verb tenses	
Parenthesis	
Full range of punctuation	

Teacher's notes and ideas

This could be linked to the story *The Cave* (see Chapter 1). It wouldn't matter which way round you teach them.

Get the pupils to be as creative as they like if they write their own version. You might need to stimulate ideas by giving them pictures of random objects and weird-looking animals to add to the ingredients.

There is an adjective list in the grammar section, which could be useful for pupils to add to their ingredients to make their text more explicit.

Table 14.2

Criteria	Examples from the text
Fronted adverbials	However, unfortunately
Preposition phrases	at one and the same time during the night with a full moon very early in the morning with the fat for 3 minutes
Formal language	Purchase (instead of 'buy'), recommend
Subordinating conjunctions / subordinate clauses	However, <u>if</u> you are lucky enough to know a good-natured dragon, then you can be generous with the spicier elements of the recipe. However, <u>before</u> you even buy or prepare this particular dish, I strongly recommend you purchase fireproof gloves <u>because</u> many of the ingredients could seriously burn your hands. <u>If</u> you are unlucky enough to know a bad-tempered dragon, then it might be better to exclude, or reduce, some of the hotter ingredients, <u>which</u> will make the dish less harmful to humans and other animals. Fluorescent blue, bulletproof vest would be a good idea <u>as</u> sometimes the ingredients can be very volatile… <u>Once</u> they've escaped, they can be very angry and sting anything or anyone in sight.
Relative clauses	…the hotter ingredients, which will make the dish less harmful to humans and other animals. It is the chillies which give the dish its red colour. Unfortunately, there are more bad-tempered dragons – who can be extremely grumpy – than good-natured ones.
Exclamation mark	You have been warned! You will need it!
Dash	Fireproof gloves – preferably arm's length, but it would be all right if they only come up to the elbow.
Hyphenated words	good-natured red-hot bad-tempered fire-eating

Co-ordinating conjunctions / co-ordinate clauses	At one and the same time, this can be a very dangerous <u>but</u> exciting event. I know this is a bit heavy <u>but</u> you're better protected than dead. This recipe has proved successful in the past <u>but</u> many people have not survived the ordeal. Heat half the slugs in the microwave for 3 minutes <u>and</u> put the other half with the fat in the oven for 15 minutes. Fluorescent blue, bulletproof vest would be a good idea as some-times the ingredients can be very volatile <u>and</u> behave like bullets from a machine gun…
Question	What do you cook a fussy, grumpy dragon for dinner?
Colons	Equipment needed, or rather essential: Ingredients for cooking: Method, or rather how to bung them all together: Danger: be careful as the microwave can cause the slugs to explode. You have been warned! Be warned: the hotter you make the dish the more irritable the dragon will become.
Commas to separate lists	At one and the same time, this can be a very dangerous but exciting event. However, before you even buy or prepare this particular dish… If you are unlucky enough to know a bad-tempered dragon, then it might be better to exclude, or reduce, some of the hotter ingredients, which will make the dish less harmful to humans and other animals. Equipment needed, or rather essential: Sprinkle the charcoal embers on top, just to add flavour.
Apostrophes for contraction	don't, you're, they've
Conditional verbs	Would, can, could, will, might
Semi-colons in a sentence	Fluorescent blue, bulletproof vest would be a good idea as some-times the ingredients can be very volatile and behave like bullets from a machine gun; this has the potential to kill the chef.
Swapping from formal to infor-mal language	Method or rather how to bung them all together: Mix in the live fire-eating ants. This can be a bit tricky because they try to escape. Once they've escaped they can be very angry and sting anything or anyone in sight.
Variety of verb tenses	can be will become buy needed prepare would could have been feeding might cover will make has proved warned

(continued)

Table 14.2 (*cont.*)

Parenthesis	400g of charcoal embers heated to exactly 51°C (don't let the temperature drop below 49°C). 50 red slugs, which have been feeding on red-hot chillies for over one month. (It is the chillies which give the dish its red colour.)
Full range of punctuation	Full stops, commas, exclamation marks, question marks, brackets, dashes, hyphens, semi-colons, colons

15   Should Children Have Been Evacuated in World War II?

Introduction

Before World War II started, the government had put plans in place to evacuate children from the major cities in the event that war broke out. The government feared that the Germans would bomb civilians in populated areas, as they had done in World War I, particularly those living near factories and industrial areas. In order to prevent the loss of thousands of children's lives, they devised and planned Operation Pied Piper, which sent children to the countryside to reside with complete strangers: a risky strategy.

Since the end of the war, people have discussed and debated whether this decision was right. Some evacuees feel very strongly that their lives were ruined and blighted, but others enjoyed the experience and met many new and interesting people who became firm friends. Indeed, in some cases, the host families were kinder and more loving than their real families at home.

Argument for staying in London

Many people would claim that staying with their parents, who would love and nurture them, naturally, allows children to grow, develop and prosper better in the home environment. It gives them confidence, security and stability, enabling them more easily to try new things, opening up more personal options and generally improving their prospects, happiness and sense of wellbeing. Love and care, parents say, is the crucial and overriding requirement in this situation.

Another issue concerned the expense involved for impoverished families, as they not only had to pay for themselves at home but also for their children in the countryside. The government forced all families, including the poorer ones, to pay for their absent children's board and lodgings and, because of this, many parents were put under financial pressure. Moreover, these payments weren't guaranteed to be spent on their own children. This situation didn't come to light until after the war when it was then revealed that many evacuated children had been fed on very basic food while the host family feasted on a varied diet – and such a varied diet was sheer luxury during the war period, for anyone.

Finally, many children were sent to places that turned out to be more dangerous than London, for example, Kent. German planes flew over Kent on their way home dropping a multitude of spare bombs on Kentish towns and villages. This resulted in many suffering massive bomb damage and thousands of people being killed. This was clearly one of many places that the government did not expect to be under threat, thus making a mockery of the evacuation strategy. Parents, therefore, seriously questioned the appropriateness and, indeed, the point of being separated from their children – along with the potential financial ruin that many of them faced – when their children were just as likely to die with their host families.

Some host families treated the evacuees unfairly and resented their being there, leaving the evacuees feeling lonely, unhappy and isolated. Many children ran away, returning to their parents, because they were being mistreated. As a result of all this, some children lost confidence and self-belief, which was inevitably carried forward into their future.

Also, some children didn't see their parents for over six years. During that time many children changed considerably as childhood is a very formative time; it is the time when a young person changes most. As a result, when they returned home, the children found it hard to become part of the family again.

People were more intolerant of differences back in the 1940s: it was deemed acceptable to be prejudiced then. So, when some children adopted different accents, such as Welsh or Cornish, families taunted and teased their children on their return. Subsequently, many families had to get to know each other again, to re-build; this took many years for some families. It was not unknown that some relationships failed to recover again – ever.

There was evidence of prejudice from some of the host families as well, especially if the evacuees were 'different'. In Pamela's story, when the host family discovered that she was Jewish, Pamela was screamed at and ordered to leave. They accused her of 'contaminating' their dishes, their knives and their forks – even the very air they breathed. This led to many Jewish children being sent back to the cities because the host families would not accept them, despite returning them to terrible danger.

Argument for moving to the countryside

Continuous bombing, for 76 days and nights with only one night of relief, meant that no one was safe from the bombs, not even in the air raid shelters. This is why the children had to go.

In one horrific story, not long after the air raid siren wailed in its monotonic tone, a stray bomb hit Balham tube station: everyone who sheltered there died – young or old, male or female, rich or poor – no one was spared. This story begs the question, isn't it better that you are unhappy but alive than die at a young age? A distraught firefighter at the Balham tube station disaster said: 'We felt totally helpless. There are times like this that we wonder why we are fighting this war but we know that we can't give in: we must fight Hitler until the very end.'

Before the war, it was considered improper for a woman to work, but the war changed all that. It was necessary for women to do men's jobs while they were away fighting. With both parents occupied and schools closed, there was no one to take care of the children. If the womenfolk had looked after the children full time, they would have been prevented from undertaking essential war work. Relying on neighbours to look after them was perilous because they too were not immune from losing their own homes and lives in the night raids. The Government used propaganda posters to recruit childminders to look after working women's children – but with limited success – because everyone was heavily occupied and vulnerable to war damage and death. No one was spared!

Another consideration was that air raid shelters could be very crowded. They were inadequate: no food, water, ventilation, sanitation or privacy. Even though people were allocated shelters, if you were not near it when the alarm was raised, you were forced to use the closest tube station. This caused chaos and even more overcrowding in some stations. What could the government do?

In the city, the air pollution was terrible, whereas in the country the air was clean and healthy: free from the smog, acrid smoke and pollution from the factories and docks. Many children in the cities died young owing to lung-related illnesses which were aggravated by the smoke and pollution. This was not the case with the evacuated children: they returned home physically healthier. So, the evacuation programme may have saved many children from an early death.

During the war, rationed food was scarce and there was not enough to feed growing children. The countryside had more available food, especially free food found on the trees, in the bushes and the farms. For many years, many children had suffered malnutrition in the cities but quickly grew stronger and healthier when they moved to the countryside with extra food being accessible. What an added bonus for hungry children!

Finally, and more importantly, many children had some fresh and exciting experiences and learnt to have a life-long love for the environment at the same time as creating life-long friendships. Both Denis and Nina (two evacuees) said they came away from the experience with a new and deep appreciation of the countryside. If the war had not happened, then some of the children, who had made really good friends, would not have had the opportunity to meet people from different backgrounds, which opened their minds and hearts.

Some evacuees were evacuated to other countries such as Canada and Australia; something that they would never have done if evacuation had not taken place. There were many touching and emotional stories on how the evacuees afterwards made their new country their home for life.

Conclusion

It is easy to look back on the evacuees' experiences and make a personal judgement as to whether or not it was the right thing to do, but the government at the time could only make decisions based on the knowledge and resources they had available to them; and it must never be forgotten that war can create forced decisions that would never normally be considered in peacetime.

I personally believe that, overall, more people had good experiences than bad ones. It is not possible to know how many children would have died if they had not been evacuated. I, therefore, maintain that evacuation was the right thing to do – although maybe it could have been handled better. I think that the people of the 1940s meant well but did not always know how to do it well. How would we do things differently if we were in the same situation now? It is hard to paint two scenarios when only one is an option for us. We only know the story of what happened, not what didn't happen.

Analyse the text

Table 15.1

Criteria	Examples from the text	
Summary of each paragraph		
Cohesive devices within and across sentences and paragraphs (including adverbials, determiners, conjunctions, pronouns and ellipses)		
Different verb forms used accurately		
Co-ordinating and subordinating conjunctions	Co-ordinating	Subordinating
Capital letters, full stops.		
Question marks		
Exclamation marks		
Commas for lists		

Apostrophes for contraction	
Selecting vocabulary and grammatical structure to reflect the level of formality	
Passive sentences	
Modal verbs	
Wide range of clause structures in varying position

Subordinate clause | |
Adverbs	
Preposition phrases	
Expanded noun phrases	
Inverted commas	

(*continued*)

Table 15.1 (cont.)

Commas for clarity	
Parenthesis (brackets)	
Semi-colons to mark the boundary between independent clauses	
Dashes	
Colons for lists	
Hyphens	
Managing shifts between levels of formality through vocabulary and grammatical structures	
Wide range of punctuation	
Colons to mark the boundary between independent clauses	

Teacher's notes and ideas

Sentences can start with a co-ordinating conjunction such as 'and', 'but', 'or', 'yet', 'so'. These forms can be used for literary effect if used sparingly and intentionally. This needs explaining when analysing the text with the pupils.

This activity can be done in conjunction with the Blitz story. It is better to do this first as this then leads into the story.

To be able to discuss the pros and cons of evacuation, the pupils will need to know the history behind it. Pick some stories that give both sides as some children really did enjoy their time as evacuees while others found it a terrible experience. There are so many stories and further information online:

> http://timewitnesses.org/evacuees/list.html
> www.historylearningsite.co.uk/world-war-two/world-war-two-in-western-europe/britains-home-front-in-world-war-two/
> www.bbc.co.uk/history/ww2peopleswar/stories/87/a2051687.shtml
> www.bbc.co.uk/schools/primaryhistory/world_war2/evacuation/

Carrie's War and *Goodnight Mr Tom* are great books to read alongside this unit.

This activity could also be used as a platform to discuss the very topical issue of immigration (why people move) and the complexity of integration from both perspectives: those receiving evacuees and those being forced to move.

Paul's Journey – NUT (www.teachers.org.uk/files/Pauls-Story-7147.pdf) is a story of a Jewish boy having to flee from Germany to the UK. This could be converted to a poem (see the poetry section for how to change from verse to prose).

> *How long ago the dangerous journey began*
> *Yet it seems that only yesterday I ran.*
> *Since then many lifetimes have been and gone.*
> *I knew then that it was all wrong.*
>
> *From Germany to England*
> *From England to Amsterdam*
> *Looking for safety*
> *Looking for a home!*

Table 15.2

Criteria	Examples from the text
Summary of each paragraph	Analysis of each paragraph: 1 Introduction – governmental plans to evacuate children in the event of war 2 Introduction – what was debated after the war 3 Parents want the best for their child 4 Parents have to pay for several lodgings – their own and their child's 5 Towns with evacuees were vulnerable and probably more dangerous 6 Summing up of the argument 7 Host families mistreated the evacuees

(continued)

Table 15.2 (*cont.*)

	8 Children changed and struggled to fit in when they returned home 9 Prejudice against Jewish children 10 76 days of bombing 11 Balham tube station story 12 No one to look after the children 13 Crowded air raid shelters 14 Countryside had cleaner air 15 More food available 16 New experiences and friends made 17 Some evacuees moved across the water to foreign lands 18 Conclusion – whether it was right or wrong 19 Conclusion – personal opinion is that it was the right thing to do; it was just not carried out in the best way.
Cohesive devices within and across sentences and paragraphs (including adverbials, determiners, conjunctions, pronouns and ellipses)	Even though people were allocated shelters, if you were not near it when the alarm was raised, you were forced to use the closest tube station. This caused chaos… ('This' refers back to the fact that many people used the closest shelter rather than an allocated one.) The government forced all families…to pay for their absent children's board and lodgings… these payments weren't guaranteed to be spent on their own children. ('these payments' refers back to parents having to pay for their child in the countryside.) Before the war, it was considered improper for a woman to work, but the war changed all that. (This is the change of attitude from before the war to during the war. Women working was a consequence of the war.) Finally, and more importantly, many children had some fresh and exciting experiences… (this point concludes the argument for moving to the countryside.)
Different verb forms used accurately	started not only had to pay mistreated had put didn't come to light had suffered would had been fed would not have had living were sent would never have done to prevent being killed have discussed were being feel would claim

Co-ordinating and subordinating conjunctions	Co-ordinating	Subordinating
	And, but	While, as, if, when, whereas, even though, despite, whether

Capital letters, full stops.	(As evidenced.)
Question marks	Should children stay in London or move to the countryside during World War II? What could the government do? How would we do things differently if we were in the same situation now?
Exclamation marks	What an added bonus for hungry children! No one was spared!

Commas for lists	It gives them confidence, security and stability...
	...'contaminating' their dishes, their knives and their forks
	...young or old, male or female, rich or poor – no one was spared.
	They were inadequate: no food, water, ventilation, sanitation or privacy.
	...from the smog, acrid smoke and pollution...
Apostrophes for contraction	didn't, weren't, shouldn't, isn't, can't
Selecting vocabulary and grammatical structure to reflect the level of formality	Before the war, it was considered improper for a woman to work, but the war changed all that.
	Another consideration was that air raid shelters could be very crowded.
	Many people would claim that staying with their parents...
	Another issue concerned the expense involved for impoverished families...
	Moreover, these payments weren't guaranteed to be spent on their own children.
	This was clearly one of many places that the government did not expect to be under threat, thus making a mockery of the evacuation strategy.
	(The final paragraph reverts to the first person to give a personal opinion on the discussion.) – I personally believe that, overall, more people had good experiences than bad ones. It is not possible to know how many children would have died if they had not been evacuated. I, therefore, maintain that evacuation was the right thing to do – although maybe it could have been handled better.
Passive sentences	...lung-related illnesses which were aggravated by the smoke and pollution.
	Pamela was screamed at and ordered to leave.
	...when the alarm was raised...
	...it was then revealed...
	...it was deemed acceptable to be prejudiced then.
	...was considered improper for a woman to work...
Modal verbs	would, should, could, can
Wide range of clause structures in varying position Subordinate clauses	Before World War II started, the government had put plans in place to evacuate children from the major cities in the event that war broke out.
	The government feared that the Germans would bomb civilians in populated areas, as they had done in World War I, particularly those living near factories and industrial areas.
	Many people would claim that staying with their parents, who would love and nurture them, naturally, allows the children to grow, develop and prosper better in the home environment.
	For many years, children had suffered malnutrition in the cities but quickly grew stronger and healthier when they moved to the countryside with extra food being accessible.

(continued)

Table 15.2 (*cont.*)

Adverbs			
	particularly	seriously	totally
	strongly	likely	heavily
	naturally	unfairly	physically
	generally	inevitably	quickly
	easily	considerably	importantly
	only	subsequently	really
	finally	especially	normally
	clearly	too	differently

Preposition phrases	during the war period from the major cities with complete strangers Since the end of the war… in this situation for their children in the countryside
Expanded noun phrases	civilians in populated areas the loss of thousands of children's lives the right thing to do some fresh and exciting experiences
Inverted commas	'We felt totally helpless. There are times like this that we wonder why we are fighting this war but we know that we can't give in: we must fight Hitler until the very end.'
Commas for clarity	The government feared that the Germans would bomb civilians in populated areas, as they had done in World War I, particularly those living near factories and industrial areas. Indeed, in some cases, the host families were kinder and more loving than their real families at home. Many people would claim that staying with their parents, who would love and nurture them, naturally, allows the children to grow, develop and prosper better in the home environment. Another issue concerned the expense involved for impoverished families, as they not only had to pay for themselves at home but also for their children in the countryside. Finally, many children were sent to places that turned out to be more dangerous than London, for example, Kent.
Parenthesis (brackets)	(two evacuees)
Semi-colons to mark the boundary between independent clauses	During that time many children changed considerably as childhood is a very formative time; it is the time when a young person changes most. Subsequently, many families had to get to know each other again, to rebuild; this took many years for some families. Some evacuees were evacuated to other countries such as Canada and Australia; something that they would never have done if evacuation had not taken place.

	It is easy to look back on the evacuees' experiences and make a personal judgement as to whether or not it was the right thing to do, but the government at the time could only make decisions based on the knowledge and resources they had available to them; and it must never be forgotten that war can create forced decisions that would never normally be considered in peacetime.
Dashes	Parents, therefore, seriously questioned the appropriateness and, indeed, the point of being separated from their children – along with the potential financial ruin that many of them faced – when their children were just as likely to die with their host families.
	…everyone who sheltered there died – young or old, male or female, rich or poor – no one was spared.
	I, therefore, maintain that evacuation was the right thing to do – although maybe it could have been handled better.
Colons for lists	They were inadequate: no food, water, ventilation, sanitation or privacy.
Hyphens	self-belief, re-build, life-long
Managing shifts between levels of formality through vocabulary and grammatical structures	The countryside had more available food, especially free food found on the trees, in the bushes and the farms. For many years, children had suffered malnutrition in the cities but quickly grew stronger and healthier when they moved to the countryside with extra food being accessible. What an added bonus for hungry children!
	(The last line is more informal.)
	Also compare the informality of the last paragraph – the author's opinion – with the formality of the rest of the discussion.
Wide range of punctuation	Exclamation mark, question mark, full stops, colons, semi-colons, brackets, commas, dashes and inverted commas.
Colons to mark the boundary between independent clauses	In order to prevent the loss of thousands of children's lives, they devised and planned Operation Pied Piper, which sent children to the countryside to reside with complete strangers: a risky strategy.
	People were more intolerant of differences back in the 1940s: it was deemed acceptable to be prejudiced then.
	In one horrific story, not long after the air raid siren wailed in its monotonic tone, a stray bomb hit Balham tube station: everyone who sheltered there died – young or old, male or female, rich or poor – no one was spared.
	A distraught firefighter at the Balham tube station disaster said: 'We felt totally helpless. There are times like this that we wonder why we are fighting this war but we know that we can't give in: we must fight Hitler until the very end.'
	They were inadequate: no food, water, ventilation, sanitation or privacy.
	In the city, the air pollution was terrible, whereas in the country the air was clean and healthy: free from the smog, acrid smoke and pollution from the factories and docks.
	This was not the case with the evacuated children: they returned home physically healthier.

16 The Argument for Quitting Social Media

Have you had enough of listening – constantly – to other people's ill-informed opinions and, subsequently, feeling upset or angry at their ignorant comments? I certainly have and that is why I'm quitting social media: or almost.

My company relies on internet communication and presence, so why am I distancing myself from something that feeds my own business interests? You may also wonder why something that is viewed with great reverence, and is given so much time, has become a burden rather than a tool to me? Quite simply, I've allowed it to happen: my responsibility. Now I'm going to take back control of my life and not allow social media and blogs to rule it. Some of you will be surprised by my decision to reverse my current practice but, before you walk away sceptical, at least give my viewpoint some airtime.

Negativity sticks to me like chewing gum to the underside of a table; it reduces my productivity and creativity. At such times, my mood becomes sour and I find I'm angry with everyone and everything. Harmful, judgemental and unenlightened material inundates social media sites such as Facebook, blogs, Snapchat and Twitter; this affects me significantly, and I find myself feeling perpetually agitated, frustrated and drained. Indeed, I now often refer to social media as 'anti-social media'.

Recently, the uproar on social media platforms has become too much to handle; it seems to me that everyone has an opinion on every event; these 'commentators' believe that the rest of us languish in dark ignorance. In this dimension, people are demonised, events misrepresented and businesses criticised: and judgements flow like waterfalls from these people of little or no knowledge. This situation has truly sent me into a downward spiral and I have had to do something to address it; so I decided to cut off the source which fed the monster. And I have done just that.

More voices out there 'in the real world' are emphasising the need to reduce or quit social media, stating that these now popular forums are counterproductive. Cal Newport's piece in the *New York Times*, for example, claims that people should quit as 'your career may depend on it' – and that it corrodes our society, indeed creating a 'cultural shallowness'.

From experience and research, I have found that there are at least three areas of life that could be vastly improved for everyone. These are:

More peace: less frustration

The need to oppose poorly researched opinions frustrates me – and social media is bursting at the seams with them. For many years, I've tried to put forward a balanced view for people to consider. Unfortunately, they see it as bait and rise to the situation to bite back. They become rude and abrasive, particularly when they can hide behind a pseudonym – feeling that they can say what they like no matter how hurtful that is or how inaccurate the information may be.

Reading the Kent Parent blog just horrifies me when you read *'Throughout the UK many thousands of parents of Year 6 children have refused to take their children to school to protest against the SATS exams. I totally agree with them. If my daughter were old enough, I would have too.'* Unfortunately, a picture of only eight people – four children and four adults – holding up three placards, supports the 'thousands' of parents. Also it must be pointed out that the UK consists of England, Northern Ireland, Scotland and Wales, and, as far as I know, Scotland and Northern Ireland don't do SATs so writing, '*Throughout the UK...*' is very misleading. I would like to know where the writer finds their information about the 'many thousands' of protestors because even the government won't have an accurate figure for this statistic, as it is, and never will be recorded. Kent Parent has simply sensationalised a sensitive situation to persuade people to support their 'take' of the argument. Unfortunately, many people don't question press statements like these. In fact, and, even worse, they pass the view on until it is in danger of becoming a national truth.

Despite the attempt by some who try to offer the funny side of life and thought-provoking words of wisdom, negativity sticks more firmly and spreads more rapidly. Educating people who offer unsubstantiated news reports is a thankless and endless task, so surely it is better not to read them in the first place. At least that would remove the necessity of banging one's head against the wall in frustration.

Removing myself from misleading stories has brought about an instant inner peace. Instead, I've surrounded myself with uplifting comments, inspiring videos, balanced reports and intelligent people. What a difference that makes!

Increased concentration: reduced distraction

My second objection to social media is that it is thought, in some circles, to be relatively harmless, whereas the opposite is surely true? Essentially, by reducing or eliminating your time focusing on social media, you leave yourself space and time to concentrate on other things that will progress your career or education or enhance your own personal development.

Before relinquishing my social media habit, I would turn to it for distraction when work was becoming difficult or confusing. It gave me an escape route, offering a diversion, but I would feel disappointed in myself later for wasting time. Hours could drift by without me actually achieving anything except being informed about other people's lives, which in themselves weren't particularly interesting either. I regret the hours spent focusing on the wrong things, simply looking the wrong way.

The ability to concentrate on hard tasks is becoming increasingly more valuable in this era of greater complexity; distraction in the form of social media, which is designed to be addictive, is readily available, weakening the skill to focus on challenging tasks. The more you use social media the more you want to use it – usually during every hour of every waking moment. You judge yourself by other people's lives: you look at what they've eaten, said or done and feel left out. With the slightest hint of boredom, you begin to reach out automatically for the phone or another electronic device to learn about other people's 'exciting' lives.

This distraction diminished my ability to concentrate on tasks that I had difficulty in finishing. Quickly, I would flick to the Facebook page to watch a video showing something mindless or read inane grumbles about someone's bad day. Why do I want to share somebody else's awful day?

I'm now free from the temptation to flick between web pages and I can focus on my selected task for longer. I am becoming more creative and can explore problems more deeply, producing better solutions and outcomes. My brain's muscles are quite literally strengthening.

Quitting social media has helped me stay in the real-life flow for extended periods of time. By staying in the flow, I achieve more and with this achievement my brain releases endorphins. These endorphins create happiness; with more happiness, my productivity increases – and this is a win-win situation.

I fear losing this ability to focus and achieve, so continuing to practice a life of addictive social media behaviour is totally abhorrent to me. It would be like an Olympic athlete drinking, smoking and eating unhealthy food while training. Why would any athlete choose to do that?

If you are serious about creating a purposeful career, then you need to step away from the toxic and addictive use of social media and blogs, which I now know harm and corrode the mind.

Now I focus on my life, not other people's.

Less pressure: more achievement

Pressure and social media are inevitably related. When you're 'hooked', there is always the pressure to share what you are thinking or doing, the pressure, constantly to do something that is noteworthy and the pressure to keep up-to-date with other people's lives in case you miss out on the latest 'fad'. As I no longer read the shallow material on social media, I don't worry that my life is less or more interesting than someone else's or that I should have an opinion on some huge global event that really doesn't interest me.

In a way, social media was invented to allow people to release pressure by having a voice and exercising it, but this modern platform has actually had the opposite effect. Bullying has increased as bullies now have access to their victims day and night. People can say vicious things and hide behind anonymity so there are no adverse consequences for them.

Stepping back from this distraction has allowed me to set and achieve goals as well as participate in life, rather than simply watching other people do that. I now compete with just myself; I want to be a better person than yesterday, rather than only being better than a friend from Facebook. I have also noticed a positive shift in my attitude and mindset. I am enjoying this new growth and can't wait to see how different everything will be living a life without social media.

Conclusion

I mentioned earlier that I will *almost* quit social media. However, I will continue to use LinkedIn, as it is a means to connect with the professional world; also it will be for my personal benefit, especially as it normally excludes the excessive behaviour frequently encountered on alternative sites.

I understand that social media has been invented and cannot be uninvented. However, it will continue to provide a forum for unacceptable comments and behaviour and it will feed and spread negativity around the world. Furthermore, shaking off the shackles of social media has given me more time to read interesting books, watch inspiring speakers, find inner peace, generate more space for creative thinking and expand my gratitude and appreciation of my immediate physical, social and spatial world.

So, abandon the social media scene and reclaim your life, stimulate your brain, elevate your spirits, and secure your future happiness.

Give it a go! You have nothing to lose and everything to gain.

Analyse the text

Table 16.1

Criteria	Examples from the text	
Paragraphs to organise ideas		
Cohesive devices within and across sentences and paragraphs (including adverbials, determiners, conjunctions, pronouns and ellipses)		
Selected verb forms for meaning and effect		
Co-ordinating and subordinating conjunctions	**Co-ordinating**	**Subordinating**
Wide range of clause structures in varying position Subordinate clauses		
Capital letters/full stops		
Question marks		
Exclamation marks		
Apostrophes for contraction		

(continued)

Table 16.1 (*cont.*)

Managing shifts between levels of formality through selecting vocabulary and manipulating grammatical structures			
Passive sentences			
Modal verbs			
Use of adverbs, preposition phrases and expanded noun phrases to add detail	Adverbs	Preposition phrases	Expanded noun phrases
Commas for lists			
Commas for clarity			
Punctuation for parenthesis			
Semi-colons to mark the boundary between independent clauses			
Dashes			
Colons			
Hyphens			

Teacher's notes and ideas

Sentences can start with a co-ordinating conjunction such as 'and', 'but', 'or', 'yet', 'so'. These forms can be used for literary effect if used sparingly and intentionally. This needs explaining when analysing the text with the pupils.

There is an opportunity to look historically at how information was disseminated. If you go back as far as the Elizabethan era, paintings were used to portray strength, wealth and good health. You can collect a selection of paintings of Elizabeth I and ask the pupils to order them from youngest to oldest. The painting depicting her in her old age is *Elizabeth I* (The Ditchley Portrait) and was painted in 1592, just over a decade before she died in 1603. This painting makes her still look young and powerful: paintings always conveyed messages through symbols; they just need to be interpreted.

A continuation of the historical slant is to look at the news coverage and how news was disseminated in the two World Wars. The government was predominantly in control of what the people heard and saw. They deliberately put a positive angle on all their communications in order to maintain morale, which was fundamental for continued support. However, some poets such as Siegfried Sassoon and Wilfred Owen wanted to communicate the horrors of the trenches and did so in their poems; see *Suicide in the Trenches* and *Dulce et Decorum Est*. Others also used poems to persuade men to enlist. See *Who's for the Game* by Jessie Pope.

This activity could also be protracted to investigate how important the English language is, and how easily it can be misunderstood, or rather manipulated, to its own end.

The article 'Quit Social Media. Your Career May Depend on It' is a real article. Again, it is another form of persuasive text. Look at real blogs and newspapers to analyse their validity. Where did people get their information from and how real are the statistics they quote? It is quite startling what people put forward as the truth when, in reality, it is just their opinion.

This activity could lead to a discussion as to whether social media does harm or whether it is good. It could be further developed by exploring the power of the word, bullying and how social media could be used to spread positivity but also lends itself to spreading negativity. Also, what is the impact when rumours and opinions are passed on as purported truths?

The PSHE Association website has created a bullet-point list on PSHE to include health and wellbeing, relationships and living in the wider world (www.pshe-association.org.uk/curriculum-and-resources/resources/programme-study-pshe-education-key-stages-1–5).

A list of the relevant points are found below.

Health and wellbeing

1 What positively and negatively affects pupils' physical, mental and emotional health.
2 How to make informed choices (including recognising that choices can have positive, neutral and negative consequences).
3 To recognise how images in the media (and online) do not always reflect reality and can affect how people feel about themselves.
4 To recognise how their increasing independence brings increased responsibility to keep themselves and others safe.
5 How pressure to behave in unacceptable, unhealthy or risky ways can come from a variety of sources, including people they know and the media.
6 To recognise when they need help and to develop the skills to ask for help; to use basic techniques for resisting pressure to do something dangerous, unhealthy, that makes them uncomfortable or anxious or that they think is wrong.
7 Strategies for keeping safe online; the importance of protecting personal information, including passwords, addresses and the distribution of images of themselves and others.

Relationships

1 To recognise what constitutes a positive, healthy relationship and develop the skills to form and maintain positive and healthy relationships.
2 To recognise ways in which a relationship can be unhealthy and whom to talk to if they need support.
3 To recognise different types of relationship, including those between acquaintances, friends, relatives and families.
4 That their actions affect themselves and others.
5 That differences and similarities between people arise from a number of factors, including family, cultural, ethnic, racial and religious diversity, age, sex, gender identity, sexual orientation, and disability (see 'protected characteristics' in the Equality Act 2010).
6 To realise the nature and consequences of discrimination, teasing, bullying and aggressive behaviours (including cyber bullying, use of prejudice-based language, 'trolling', how to respond and ask for help).
7 To recognise and challenge stereotypes.
8 How to recognise bullying and abuse in all its forms (including prejudice-based bullying both in person, online and through social media).
9 To understand personal boundaries; to identify what they are willing to share with their most special people; friends; classmates and others; and that we all have rights to privacy.

Living in the wider world

1 To research, discuss and debate topical issues, problems and events that are of concern to them and offer their recommendations to appropriate people.
2 To realise the consequences of anti-social, aggressive and harmful behaviours such as bullying and discrimination of individuals and communities; to develop strategies for getting support for themselves or for others at risk.
3 To resolve differences by looking at alternatives, seeing and respecting others' points of view, making decisions and explaining choices.
4 **To critically examine what is presented to them in social media and why it is important to do so; understand how information contained in social media can misrepresent or mislead; the importance of being careful what they forward to others.**

Table 16.2

Criteria	Examples from the text
Paragraphs to organise ideas	(As evidenced.)
Cohesive devices within and across sentences and paragraphs (including adverbials, determiners, conjunctions, pronouns and ellipses)	My company relies on internet communication and presence, so why am I distancing myself from <u>something</u> that feeds my own business interests? ('something' relates back to the internet communication.) Negativity sticks to me like chewing gum to the underside of a table; <u>it</u> reduces my productivity and creativity. ('it' relates back to negativity.) Harmful, judgemental and unenlightened material inundates social media sites such as Facebook, blogs, Snapchat and Twitter; <u>this</u> affects me significantly, and I find myself feeling perpetually agitated, frustrated and drained. ('this' relates back to 'harmful...') I certainly have and that is why I'm quitting social media: or almost. (First paragraph) <u>Now</u> I'm going to take back control of <u>my life</u> and not allow social media and blogs to rule <u>it</u>. (Second paragraph – 'now' states the immediacy of quitting from the first paragraph. The pronoun 'it' refers back to 'my life'.) See sections below for conjunctions and adverbs.

Selected verb forms for meaning and effect	have also noticed am enjoying was invented to allow has increased should have would be would any athlete choose has helped diminished is becoming	is designed to be gave would feel disappointed being informed I've surrounded give has been invented will continue to provide shaking off has allowed
Co-ordinating and subordinating conjunctions	**Co-ordinating** and but so	**Subordinating** when because before until whereas
Wide range of clause structures in varying position Subordinate clauses	Before relinquishing my social media habit, I would turn to it for distraction when work was becoming difficult or confusing. Some of you will be surprised by my decision to reverse my current practice but, before you walk away sceptical, at least give my viewpoint some air space. Despite the attempt by some who try to offer the funny side of life and thought-provoking words of wisdom, negativity sticks more firmly and spreads more rapidly. I would like to know where the writer finds her information about the 'thousands' of protestors because even the government won't have an accurate figure for this statistic, as it is, and never will be recorded.	
Capital letters/full stops	(As evidenced.)	
Question marks	Have you had enough of listening – constantly – to other people's ill-informed opinions and, subsequently, feeling upset or angry at their ignorant comments? You may also wonder why something that is viewed with great reverence and is given so much time, has become a burden rather than a tool to me? My second objection to social media is that it is thought, in some circles, to be relatively harmless, whereas the opposite is surely true? Why do I want to share somebody else's awful day?	
Exclamation marks	What a difference that makes! Give it a go!	
Apostrophes for contraction	I'm, I've, don't, won't, weren't, they've, you're, doesn't, can't	

(continued)

Table 16.2 (*cont.*)

Managing shifts between levels of formality through selecting vocabulary and manipulating grammatical structures	(The first paragraph contains a rhetorical question to challenge and raise interest using informality and the answer is written in the first person.) Have you had enough of listening – constantly – to other people's ill-informed opinions and, subsequently, feeling upset or angry at their ignorant comments? I certainly have and that is why I'm quitting social media: or almost. Cal Newport's piece in the *New York Times* claims that people should quit as 'your career may depend on it' – and that it corrodes our society creating a '*cultural shallowness*'. (Formal vocabulary.) (The text ends very informally.) – Give it a go! You have nothing to lose and everything to gain.
Passive sentences	In this dimension, people are demonised, events misrepresented and businesses criticised… My second objection to social media is that it is thought, in some circles, to be relatively harmless… …social media was invented to allow people to release pressure…
Modal verbs	would, should, can, will, could, must

Use of adverbs, preposition phrases and expanded noun phrases to add detail	Adverbs		Preposition phrases	Expanded noun phrases
	constantly	rapidly	at such times	appreciation of
	subsequently	surely	with great reverence	my immediate
	certainly	relatively	for people to consider	physical, social and
	simply	essentially	into the open	spatial world.
	perpetually	surely	in the first place	other people's
	significantly	actually	in dark ignorance	'exciting' lives
	recently	increasingly	on challenging tasks	a means to con-
	truly	usually		nect with the
	vastly	readily		professional world
	poorly	automatically		the temptation to flick
	unfortunately	quickly		between web pages
	particularly	deeply		more time to read
	completely	literally		interesting books,
	unfortunately	totally		watch inspiring
	only	inevitably		speakers, find inner
	firmly	normally		peace, generate
	simply	frequently		more space for cre-
	now			ative thinking

Commas for lists	Facebook, blogs, Snapchat and Twitter… Harmful, judgemental and unenlightened material… …uplifting comments, sensible videos, balanced reports and intelligent people.
Commas for clarity	Before relinquishing my social media habit, I would turn to it for distraction when work was becoming difficult or confusing.

Punctuation for parenthesis	Cal Newport's piece in the *New York Times* claims that people should quit as 'your career may depend on it' – and that it corrodes our society creating a *'cultural shallowness'*. See *Commas for clarity* and *Dashes* for further examples.
Semi-colons	Negativity sticks to me like chewing gum to the underside of a table; it reduces my productivity and creativity. Harmful, judgemental and unenlightened material inundates social media sites such as Facebook, blogs, Snapchat and Twitter; this affects me significantly, and I find myself feeling perpetually agitated, frustrated and drained. Recently, the uproar on social media platforms has become too much to handle; it seems to me that everyone has an opinion on every event; these 'commentators' believe that the rest of us languish in dark ignorance. This situation has truly sent me into a downward spiral and I have had to do something to address it; so I decided to cut off the source which fed the monster. The ability to concentrate on hard tasks is becoming increasingly more valuable in this era of greater complexity; distraction in the form of social media, which is designed to be addictive, is readily available, weakening the skill to focus on challenging tasks. However, I will continue to use LinkedIn, as it is a means to connect with the professional world; also it will be for my personal benefit, especially as it normally excludes the excessive behaviour frequently encountered on alternative sites.
Dashes	Have you had enough of listening – constantly – to other people's ill-informed opinions and, subsequently... the *New York Times* claims that people should quit as 'your career may depend on it' – and that it corrodes our society, indeed creating a *'cultural shallowness'*. The need to oppose poorly researched opinions frustrates me – and social media is bursting at the seams with them. They become rude and abrasive, particularly when they can hide behind a pseudonym – feeling that they can say what they like no matter how hurtful that is or how inaccurate the information may be. Unfortunately, a picture of only eight people – five children and three adults – holding up three placards... These endorphins create happiness, with more happiness, my productivity increases – and this is a win-win situation.
Colons	I certainly have and that is why I'm quitting social media: or almost. Quite simply, I've allowed it to happen: my responsibility. In this dimension, people are demonised, events misrepresented and businesses criticised: and judgements flow like waterfalls from these people of little or no knowledge. From experience and research, I have found that there are at least three areas of life that could be vastly improved for everyone. These are: You judge yourself by other people's lives: you look at what they've eaten, said or done and feel left out.
Hyphens	ill-informed anti-social up-to-date

17　How Did the Ancient Egyptians Mummify Their Dead?

Mummification seems a little strange for us today but we have different beliefs now and global culture has changed considerably over 4,000 years. Also, some of the mummification methods appear a little gruesome although once you're dead it's the least of your worries.

It's important to remember that the story of mummification has been handed down to us by the ancient Egyptians without our being able to speak to them. We have learnt about their methods by using modern technology to investigate artefacts discovered in recent times and we will continue to learn more with the invention of further new scientific methods.

How do we know about mummification in Ancient Egypt?

The Ancient Egyptians have left behind an abundance of evidence relating to their beliefs and culture: this has shown us what a truly remarkable and fascinating people they were.

Archaeologists have unearthed artefacts – primary resources – and many of these clues can be seen in many of the towns and cities of present day Egypt and a multitude of museums. From the artefacts such as rare and ornate walking sticks to magnificent tombs we have found out so much about how the Ancient Egyptians lived and died through this legacy.

Why the Ancient Egyptians mummified the dead

Ancient Egyptians believed in an afterlife. For this to be reached, the body had to be mummified. The mummification process was the method that allowed the body to be arranged in human form by preserving its shape and preventing the decaying process.

Who was mummified?

As the process so expensive, only the wealthy were mummified, although some poorer people were mummified. This did not mean that the poor could not move on to the afterlife as it was believed that if they recanted the spells this would be sufficient. Even though it normally took 70 days to fully prepare a body for burial, a person with lesser means would have been mummified in less than a week. It is thought that the cost of properly mummifying a body was beyond the average person's purse.

Who mummified the body?

The chief embalmer would have been a priest wearing a mask of Anubis – the jackal-headed god of the dead.

How to mummify (only for the brave-hearted)

Having discovered forensic evidence in the tombs, scientists now think they know how the body was embalmed, wrapped and buried.

First the body was transported to the west side of the Nile, where the place of purification was located: this is called the Ibu. On arrival, the embalmer pushed a hook up the nose, jiggled it about to break up the brain and allowed the contents to be removed and thrown away: it was believed that the brain was not important. The skull was then filled with either sawdust or resin (a sticky substance from trees). For the embalmers to remove the moist parts of the body and treat them with natron salt – to prevent rotting, an incision was made down the left side of the body near the stomach and the internal organs were removed to dry out in the canopic jars. There were four canopic jars; each one guarded different organs (see below for more detail). The only organ which was placed back into the body was the heart. The heart was left in the mummy in order to be weighed against the 'Feather of Truth and Justice' in the afterlife.

For the deceased to pass in to the afterlife the heart needed to weigh the same as the feather. If the heart was heavier it was deemed that the person had committed acts that were not fit for the afterlife and as a result could not pass on.

To ensure that the body did not decay, the priest rinsed the inside of the body with palm wines and spices; he packed the body with straw or dried grass to ensure it kept its shape and then covered the corpse with natron salt for 70 days to dry out. After 40 days, it was stuffed with linen or sand to give it a more human shape. At this point, the embalmers sealed the cut with wax or resin and placed a Two Fingers Amulet on it for protection. On the 70th day the embalmers then wrapped the body in linen bandages from head to toe; spells and rituals were performed to ensure that safe passage was given. The body was then fitted with a mask and placed in a sarcophagus (coffin). If the person had been a pharaoh, he would have been buried inside a special burial chamber with a mountain of treasure. Some pharaohs were buried in pyramids but thieves stole their treasures so further pharaohs were secretly buried in chambers not easily accessible.

The 'Opening of the Mouth' ceremony took place just before the burial. The priest would have touched the sarcophagus to enable the deceased to breathe again, restore speech, sight and hearing thus bringing back all the senses.

Canopic jars

The jars were the containers that housed the dried internal organs, which were then buried in the chamber with the deceased. The four sons of Horus, god of the sky, were represented on each canopic jar. They included Imsety (guards the liver), Quebhesneuf (protects the intestines), Hapy (watches over the lungs) and Duamutef (the keeper of the stomach).

Treasures of the mummies

Mummies were buried with many different types of objects placed in the sarcophagus.

Amulets were used by Ancient Egyptians to protect themselves in their daily lives, therefore it was then seen to be important for the dead to be buried with them as well. Amulets such as 'The Eye of Horus' (or wedjat eye) was a symbol of protection against evil. This amulet was placed on the heart for the 'weighing of the heart' ceremony.

Shabitas, which are turquoise figures of slaves or soldiers, were buried in the tomb of the deceased to serve him in his afterlife; it was believed that they would come to life when the deceased passed into the afterlife.

Jewellery and treasures were buried in case the dead person needed them. They were usually made of gold, particularly if the person was rich. Symbols were carved on them as this was thought to bring the owner good fortune.

In 1922, Howard Carter discovered the tomb of Tutankhamun. This tomb was filled with golden treasures that informed us about how the young king lived and what he was like as a person. Even his sarcophagus was made of gold and lapis lazuli (a blue colour stone). Gold represented Ra (the sun god) while lapis lazuli was thought to have imitated the heavens.

Elaborate and opulent furniture, models of farmers, bakers, millers and pottery have all been found in burial sites. These were everyday items that the deceased needed to have to ensure a comfortable afterlife.

Conclusion

The afterlife was as important to the Ancient Egyptians as their lives on earth. Many wealthy Egyptians could afford the lengthy mummification process but there were many more who could not pay for such an expensive practice. Because of the way the Egyptians embodied their beliefs in their culture and artistic activities, we now know about how they lived and what they believed in through objects and writings placed in their tombs. For that we thank the Ancient Egyptians for such foresight.

Analyse the text

Table 17.1

Criteria	Examples from the text	
Cohesive devices within and across sentences and paragraphs (including adverbials, determiners, conjunctions, pronouns and ellipses)		
Different verb forms		
Co-ordinating and subordinating conjunctions	**Co-ordinating**	**Subordinating**
Capital letters and full stops		
Question marks		
Commas for lists		
Apostrophes for contraction		
Selecting vocabulary and grammatical structures that reflect the level of formality		
Passive sentences		

(continued)

Table 17.1 (*cont.*)

Modal verbs			
Wide range of clause structures in varying position Subordinate clauses			
Use of adverbs, preposition phrases and expanded noun phrases to add detail	Adverbs	Preposition phrases	Expanded noun phrases
Commas for clarity			
Punctuation for parenthesis (brackets) See *Commas for clarity* section for further punctuation for parenthesis			
Semi-colons to mark the boundary between independent clauses			
Colons			
Hyphens			
Managing shifts of formality			

Teacher's notes and ideas

Some explanation texts are written in the present tense and some in the past tense. And sometimes a text is written using the past and present tense. It all depends on what is being explained.

Look at other explanation texts which are written in the present tense; could they have been written in the past? Look at this text; would it sound correct if it was changed to the present tense? Having tried it, it sounds very odd because the process of mummification used to be done and is no longer practised.

Pupils confuse the difference between instructional texts and explanation texts. To help them, you could compare this text with the dragon recipe. As a comparison, you could ask the pupils to write an explanation text on how to look after a dragon or any other mythical beast.

Table 17.2

Criteria	Examples from the text	
Cohesive devices within and across sentences and paragraphs (including adverbials, determiners, conjunctions, pronouns and ellipses)	… the west side of the Nile, where the place of purification was located: this is called the Ibu. ('this' relates back to purification place) This tomb was filled with golden treasures that informed us about how the young king lived… Archaeologists have unearthed artefacts – primary resources – and many of these clues can be seen in many of the towns and cities of present day Egypt… ('these' refers back to the artefacts)	
Different verb forms	(This explanation text lends itself to many different forms. Because the ritual of mummification happened in the past, the text is written in the past tense. However, there are points where the present tense is more applicable. This is an opportunity to explore with the pupils how verb tense can change and where it changes.)	
	seems has changed to remember has been handed down have learnt will continue to learn can be seen lived and died believed	had to be preserving could not afford would have been mummified thought discovered was transported is were removed to dry out
Co-ordinating and subordinating conjunctions	Co-ordinating	Subordinating
	and but so for	therefore although even though as because
Capital letters and full stops	(As evidenced.)	
Question marks	How did the Ancient Egyptians mummify their dead? How do we know about mummification in Ancient Egypt? Who was mummified? Who mummified the body?	

(continued)

Table 17.2 (*cont.*)

Commas for lists	Elaborate and opulent furniture, models of farmers, bakers, millers and pottery
Apostrophes for contraction	you're it's
Selecting vocabulary and grammatical structures that reflect the level of formality	...global culture has changed considerably over 4,000 years. ...mummification methods appear... It's important to remember that... ...an abundance of evidence relating to their beliefs and culture Archaeologists have unearthed artefacts... ...where the place of purification was located: this is called the Ibu.
Passive sentences	The mummification process was the method that allowed the body to be arranged in human form by preserving its shape and preventing the decaying process. Mummification was mainly performed on wealthy people... First the body was transported to the west side of the Nile... The skull was then filled with either sawdust or resin (a sticky substance from trees). ...an incision was made down the left side of the body near the stomach ...it was stuffed with linen or sand to give it a more human shape. The body was then fitted with a mask and placed in a sarcophagus (coffin).
Modal verbs	could, would, can, will
Wide range of clause structures in varying position Subordinate clauses	Also, some of the mummification methods appear a little gruesome, although once you're dead it's the least of your worries. Even though it normally took 70 days to fully prepare a body for burial, a person with lesser means would have been mummified in less than a week. Having discovered forensic evidence in the tombs, scientists now think they know how the body was embalmed, wrapped and buried. First the body was transported to the west side of the Nile, where the place of purification was located: this is called the Ibu.

Use of adverbs, preposition phrases and expanded noun phrases to add detail	Adverbs	Preposition phrases	Expanded noun phrases
	considerably truly mainly fully properly normally only secretly easily particularly usually	For this to be reached First the body was transported On arrival, For the embalmers to remove the moist parts of the body and treat them with natron salt – to prevent rotting, ...for 70 days to dry out After 40 days In 1922,	a little strange for us today some of the mummification methods their methods by using modern technology to investigate artefacts a truly remarkable and fascinating people these clues the towns and cities of present day Egypt the method that allowed the body to be arranged in human form by preserving its shape

Commas for clarity	For this to be reached, the body had to be mummified. Even though it normally took 70 days to fully prepare a body for burial, a person with lesser means would have been mummified in less than a week. Having discovered forensic evidence in the tombs, scientists now think they know how the body was embalmed, wrapped and buried. On arrival, the embalmer pushed a hook up the nose, jiggled it about to break up the brain and allowed the contents to be removed and thrown away: it was believed that the brain was not important.
Punctuation for paren- thesis (brackets and dashes) See *Commas for clar- ity* section for fur- ther punctuation for parenthesis	(only for the brave-hearted) (a sticky substance from trees) (see below for more detail) (coffin) (protects the intestines)
Semi-colons to mark the boundary between independent clauses	To ensure that the body did not decay, the priest rinsed the inside of the body with palm wines and spices; he packed the body with straw or dried grass to ensure it kept its shape and then covered the corpse with natron salt for 70 days to dry out. On the 70th day the embalmers then wrapped the body in linen bandages from head to toe; spells and rituals were performed to ensure that safe passage was given. Shabitas, which are turquoise figures of slaves or soldiers, were buried in the tomb of the deceased to serve him in his afterlife; it was believed that they would come to life when the deceased passed into the afterlife. There were four canopic jars; each one guarded different organs (see below for more detail).
Colons	The Ancient Egyptians have left behind an abundance of evidence relating to their beliefs and culture: this has shown us what a truly remarkable and fascinating people they were. First the body was transported to the west side of the Nile, where the place of purification was located: this is called the Ibu. On arrival, the embalmer pushed a hook up the nose, jiggled it about to break up the brain and allowed the contents to be removed and thrown away: it was believed that the brain was not important.
Hyphens	jackal-headed brave-hearted
Managing shifts of formality	Also, some of the mummification methods appear a little gruesome, although once you're dead it's the least of your worries. (*Informal*) For that we thank the Ancient Egyptians for such foresight. (*Informal*) Symbols were carved on them as this was thought to bring the owner good fortune. (*Formal*) The four sons of Horus, god of the sky, were represented on each canopic jar. (*Formal*)

PART III

Poetry

18   Using Poetry to Teach Grammar, Sentence Structure and Figurative Language

Poetry is an excellent mechanism to teach grammar, sentence structure and syntax. It supports the introduction of new vocabulary and provides an opportunity to learn and practise figurative language. Below is a selection of instructions and examples to use in class. Expand on the ideas and mix and match the different ones to create a variety of poems.

Grammar

Pupils struggle with word class, understandably, considering how some words belong to different word classes, such as the word 'set'. This three-letter word has nearly 200 definitions, it can be a verb, noun or an adjective. Pupils have to understand that the word class depends upon where the word is found in the sentence. By combining the study of grammar and sentence structure, the pupils rehearse and recognise different word classes.

The ideas in the following bullet-point list can either be used to create a poem in its entirety, as demonstrated below, or be used as elements of a poem.

Some ideas to support pupils' learning:

- Create lists of different word classes for pupils to use in their poems. Give them a wider list of a word class such as adverbs, and ask them to choose between 10 and 20 from the list for that poem. This facilitates introducing new vocabulary and gives pupils a chance to decide on the appropriateness of that vocabulary for its purpose. This approach will cover the 2016 Key Stage 2 English Writing Exemplification 'selecting vocabulary and grammatical structures that reflect the level of formality required mostly correctly' and areas of 'using adverbs, preposition phrases and expanded noun phrases effectively to add detail, qualification and precision'.
- Use expanded noun phrases – determiner + adjective + noun + preposition phrase – *The menacing tornado amidst the valley of fear*. These can then be used in poetry format.
- Think about the use of verbs – a verb, or possibly three verbs, could then start the next line, e.g. *Screaming, destroying, demolishing*. These words could be chosen from the word list that has been created by the teacher and possibly added to by the pupils.
- Select the adverbs carefully – an adverb could be added to each verb to make three short separate lines – *Screaming crazily, destroying eagerly, demolishing maliciously*.
- Start with an adjective to describe an abstract noun + simple present tense verb – *A terrifying blackness descends*.
- Start a line with the continuous verb tense – *Racing through the minds and ghostly souls*.
- Start with a preposition – *Of the valley's descendants*.

> The menacing tornado amidst the valley of fear
> Screaming crazily,
> Destroying eagerly,
> Demolishing maliciously,

> Racing through the minds and ghostly souls
> Of the valley's descendants
> A terrifying blackness descends.

- You can create your own order. Just be mindful of what you want to teach and what you have already taught so you can build on it. So:

> Racing through the minds and ghostly souls
> Of the valley's descendants
> The menacing tornado amidst the valley of fear
> A terrifying blackness descends
> Screaming crazily,
> Destroying eagerly,
> Demolishing maliciously.

- The poem looks at the appropriateness of the adverbs to the verbs and how the adjectives 'terrifying' and 'menacing' link with the verbs 'screaming', 'destroying' and 'demolishing'.
- There is also a link between the adjective 'ghostly' and 'descendants'.
- Note also that there is less emphasis on adjectives.
- Using this very short poem, you can teach apostrophes for possession, appropriateness of vocabulary within and across lines, noun phrases, continuous verb tense, present tense, prepositions, abstract nouns, commas for lists, length of each line and create a chance to experiment with vocabulary.

The following ideas combine sentence structure with figurative language.

Sentence structure and figurative language

Definitions of figurative language

Many of these can be used to analyse poetry as well as write it.

- Onomatopoeia – words which describe the sound they make, e.g. *snap, crackle and pop*.
- Simile – comparing an object or an idea using 'like' or 'as', e.g. *As slow as a glacier* or *like a slow glacier*.
- Personification – animals or objects are given human characteristics, e.g. *The trees reached out to grab the terrified hobbits; Fear ran riot through the minds of the waiting soldiers*.
- Metaphor – draws a verbal picture and states what something is, whereas a simile states that it is like it. Metaphors are more positive – they don't just compare things; they say one thing is another and use the word 'is' to strengthen the comparison, e.g. *Curiosity is a magical world waiting to be discovered*.
- Alliteration – each word starts with the same letter. Not every word has to start with the same letter unless you are trying to emphasise the point; sometimes it needs to be more subtle, e.g. *The tortuous tornado tore through the trees. Flying freely through the carefree clouds.* Care has to be taken to ensure that the alliteration enhances the style and effectiveness of the sentence and is not simply 'showy', too deliberately applied or self-conscious. It should be pleasing to the reader, particularly when read aloud.
- Hyperbole – an exaggeration that is obviously untrue yet, again, it should enhance the impact and emphasise the meaning of the sentence, e.g. *It is so cold that I saw a polar bear wearing a thick coat, scarf, gloves and a woolly hat*.
- Idiom – *The Cambridge Dictionary* states that an idiom is 'a group of words in a fixed order that have a particular meaning that is different from the meanings of each word on its own'. For example, *I'm all*

ears or *at the drop of a hat*. Also, it is a way of speaking within the framework of a main language that is natural or peculiar to a particular group of people or locality.

- Cliché – a saying that has been so overused that it has lost its impact and, as a result, has become boring and nearly meaningless. For example, *at the speed of light*.

Sentence structure for poetry ideas

Poetry is an excellent forum to teach sentence structure and for pupils to rehearse it and play with new vocabulary. For each point, you could either write a complete poem or mix and match as above.

1 Start each line with a preposition phrase followed by a comma. For example, 'Beneath the dark grey skies, bored commuters scurry like ants to work'. Give pupils a painting or photograph as the stimulus. Extract the nouns that can be seen or could be in the painting but are not obvious; use word banks to decide appropriate verbs, adverbs and adjectives to supplement pupils' sentences. You will need to teach prepositions and give them a list of a variety of prepositions. Include 'amidst', 'amid' and any other poetical versions. Don't forget that there are two types of prepositions: one denoting time; the other place.
2 Start a line with a subordinating conjunction – *After the clock stopped, the ghosts awoke.*
3 Start a line with two adjectives separated with either a comma, 'and' or 'but' – *Scared, terrified...*, *Scared and terrified...* or *Frightened but determined....*
4 Start a line with two adverbs – *Nervously, shyly...*, *Nervously and shyly...* or *Nervously but deliberately...*
5 Use a co-ordinating conjunction to start the next line.

> The light danced
> And the trees laughed.
> The shed sang
> But the plants cried.
> The earth listened
> Yet it could not hear.
> The foxes watched
> So the rabbits hid.

19   Angry Earth

Courage danced over the cracked earth.
Crackle, rattle, sizzle
Lava is a flowing flame weaving through the land.
Smoke jumps high into the air,
Like a kite playing with the wind.
Whish, swish, swoosh
Exploding mountains release their stress.
Terrified animals run for their lives.
Suddenly, all is quiet, quiet and calm
But never the same.

Teacher's notes

Each line of the poem uses figurative language except one – and it is this line which therefore achieves greater impact and consolidates the fundamental meaning and intention of the sentence.

Courage danced over the cracked earth. (*Personification*)
Crackle, rattle, sizzle (*Onomatopoeia*)
Lava is a flowing flame weaving through the land (*Metaphor*)
Smoke jumps high into the air (*Personification*)
Like a kite playing with the wind (*Simile*)
Whish, swish, swoosh (*Onomatopoeia*)
Exploding mountains release their stress (*Personification*)
Terrified animals run for their lives.
Suddenly, all is quiet, quiet and calm (*Repetition*)
But never the same. (*Short last line*)

20   The Island

Loosely based on ideas by Pie Corbett

The streets of foxes
Slyly and cautiously stalking
Through the sleeping city
Like a searching ghost
Looking for its prey.

The ocean of dolphins
Deliberately, elegantly skimming
Across the shimmering waves
Like a speeding train
Cutting through the land.

The island of tortoises
Slowly and clumsily moving
Over the blackened earth
Like a glacial river
Wandering aimlessly.

Teacher's notes

This table analyses the pattern of the poem for each line so that it can be replicated.

Table 20.1

Line	Format	Example
1	Determiner + place + of + animal	The ocean of dolphins
2	Two adverbs + continuous verb	Deliberately + elegantly + skimming
3	Preposition phrase	Across the dancing waves
4	Simile	Like a speeding train
5	Continuous verb	Cutting through the land

21 If I Were...

If I were bold, I would invite the Queen to dinner.
If I were a great leader, I would unite countries with friendship.
If I were more selfless, I would share my kind thoughts.
If I were more courageous, I would journey into space to visit other planets.
If I were an explorer, I would dive deep into the Mariana Trench.

Teacher's notes

This poem gives the pupils practice at identifying the subjunctive mood – in this example, the conditional subjunctive. You can create some more adjectives and adverbs to say what you would do if you had one of the traits demonstrated above. The examples also consolidate the usage of the modal verb 'would', which implies possibility (in these examples, 'would' is used to express the possibility of doing something if you had a particular characteristic) and emphasises the correct (often ignored in speech) conditional use of the subjunctive.

22   I Wish...

I wish I were a humpback whale
so I could travel from the Arctic to the Antarctic
Exploring the icy ocean depths.

I wish I could meet a hyena
and learn its laugh.

I wish I could tap dance
with an elephant in a tutu,
just to see whether he has rhythm.

I wish I could explore the ruins of Athens
to learn the lives of ancient people,
who taught us how to reach for the stars.

I wish I could trek through the Himalayas
and hear the sound of silence,
as it gently surrounds you.

Teacher's notes

This is an exercise in the use of the modal verb 'could' to show the possibility of achieving an action or an outcome in real terms.

This piece could be used in a unit of work dealing with worldwide travel, visiting different places and encountering wild animals and be used to create fresh descriptions using grammatical conventions.

The grammar included is co-ordinating and subordinating conjunctions, relative clauses and prepositions to start new lines.

23 Men of the Docks: Painting by George Bellows (1912)

This poem is about building up sentences by changing a word, adding phrases or changing the order of the lines. It is a great exercise for pupils to understand what a sentence is, to understand word class and how sentences can be manipulated.

The stimulus was the painting *Men of the Docks* by George Bellows, owned by the National Gallery. You can access the painting through the National Gallery's website.

Building the sentence

Men stand by the water.
Men wait by the water.
Men wait by the docks.
Workers wait by the docks.
Workers wait patiently by the docks.
Workers stare vacantly into the distance.
On a cold winter's day, workers stare vacantly into the distance.
On a freezing winter's day, workers stare vacantly into the distance.
Cold and wintery, workers stare vacantly into the distance.

Explore what is happening in each sentence.

Building the sentence

Ships float on the river.
Ocean liners float on the river.
Ocean liners float in the bay.
Ocean liners journey across the bay.
Ocean liners disappear across the bay.
Ocean liners disappear across the Hudson.
Ocean liners disappear across the Hudson towards the unknown.
Ocean liners disappear towards the unknown.

Take some of the lines from each section to start a poem.

Cold and wintery,
Workers stare vacantly into the distance.
Ocean liners disappear towards the unknown.

Teacher's notes

Men stand by the water (*Start with a simple short sentence using the painting as a stimulus. Change the verb*)

Men wait by the water (*Change the object of the sentence – noun*)

Men wait by the docks (*Change the subject of the sentence – noun*)

Workers wait by the docks (*Add an adverb*)

Workers wait patiently by the docks (*Keep the same format but change each word class – verb, adverb, preposition, noun phrase*)

Workers stare vacantly into the distance. (*Add a preposition phrase*)

On a cold winter's day, workers stare vacantly into the distance (*Change the adjective to create a colder image*)

On a freezing winter's day, workers stare vacantly into the distance (*Use two adjectives to shorten the sentence*)

Cold and wintery, workers stare vacantly into the distance.

Ships float on the river. (*Start with a simple short sentence using the painting as a stimulus. Change the subject – noun*)

Ocean liners float on the river. (*Change the object of the sentence – noun*)

Ocean liners float in the bay. (*By changing the verb it means you need to change the preposition phrase otherwise it doesn't make sense*)

Ocean liners journey across the bay. (*Change the verb*)

Ocean liners disappear across the bay. (*Change the subject – noun – to be more specific*)

Ocean liners disappear across the Hudson (*Add a preposition phrase*)

Ocean liners disappear across the Hudson towards the unknown. (*Shorten the sentence*)

Ocean liners disappear towards the unknown.

24 Peace

How can we bear to live without peace?
But we do.
Peace reaches out to us and we choose to ignore it.
It does not hide from us, yet we must seek it.
It speaks in silence, so we must learn to listen.
Yet hearing seems elusive.
Peace does not disguise itself and yet we do not recognise it.
Our souls are travelling too far away,
From the heart of peace.
Anger, jealousy and hate prevail too readily.
Living in angst – and at what cost to our earthly lives?
When will we realise that we deserve peace?
Just because we are.
Sharing peace is a gift,
A gift so easy to give with love
Yet it is seems intangible, indefinable, ethereal.
Now is the time to reconcile our differences both within and without.
Now is the time to forgive ourselves and others.
Now is the time to let peace be our life-long companion.

Teacher's notes

How can we bear to live without peace? (*Starts with a rhetorical question*)

But we do. (*Keep your answer short*)

Peace reaches out to us and we choose to ignore it. (*Personification*)

It does not hide from us, yet we must seek it. (*A contradiction signalled by the use of the co-ordinating conjunction 'yet'*)

It speaks in silence, so we must learn to listen. (*The co-ordinating conjunction 'so' creates a consequence of peace speaking*)

Yet hearing seems elusive. (*Repetition of 'yet'*)

Peace does not disguise itself and yet we do not recognise it. (*Personification with another contradiction*)

Our souls are travelling too far away,

From the heart of peace. (*Preposition phrase*)

Anger, envy and hate prevails too readily. (*Three abstract nouns – for emphasis*)

Living in angst – and at what cost to our earthly lives?

When will we realise that we deserve peace? (*Rhetorical question*)

Just because we are. (*Short answer*)

Sharing peace is a gift. (*Starts with a continuous verb*)

A gift so easy to give with love. (*Further explanation of the gift*)

Yet it is seems intangible, indefinable, ethereal. (*Three adjectives to mirror the three abstract nouns*)

Now is the time to reconcile our differences both within and without.

Now is the time to forgive ourselves and others.

Now is the time to let peace be our life-long companion. (*Last three lines exhibit repetition of 'Now is the time…'*)

25 A Winter's Morning: Poetry to Prose

Loosely based on ideas by Pie Corbett

It was early; very early, too early.
Leaving the warmth of my bed
The cat watched me go
He always did.

Sighing, I looked outside
Frost, ice, snow clung to the world
Winter had arrived.

With iciness in my fingers,
I fumbled for my mittens
Not there, lost.

Scraping the bitter frost,
That layered the windscreen,
A gentle breeze momentarily wandered down the street.
Freezing my bones, my soul, my thoughts
Then faded away.

Street lights cut through the darkness
As the sun struggles to emerge
Reluctant to show itself.

Nothing stirs – birds' songs have vanished.
Stillness is overwhelming,
Silent sugar-coated fields reach out over the horizon.
Deer forage
Finding the last remnants of grass
Ignoring the cold.

Wafting through the air,
Wood smoke pervades my nostrils
Reminds me of warmth
Of love, of family.

Model writing to expand the poem to prose

A Winter's Morning: Prose

This story starts very early, too early for most people. To be exact it starts at 5.15am on a cold winter's morning. Saying goodbye to the cat, I closed the front door wishing I were still snuggled up in bed. I sighed deeply as I looked across at the ice-covered car. Yet again I had to scrape the thin skin of frost from the windscreen. Searching in my pocket, I realised that I had left my mittens in the house or were they lost again? This meant my frozen fingers, numb from the cold, would fumble with the scraper and spray. A chilling wind travelled, with its own purpose, down the road and wrapped itself around me, its bitterness entering my bones and chilling my soul. And then it vanished.

Taking a short break, I looked across the sugar-coated hills, fields and hedgerows; everything had a gentle sifting of snow. The deer were foraging through the thin sheet of frost to munch at the last remnants of grass. They seemed totally unaware that their fur was frozen. Everything was so cold and so frosty that even the birds had packed up and gone. Not a tweet was heard; there was absolute silence and, with it, peace. At that moment, I thought how lucky I was to live here.

The sun had abandoned us that morning so I returned to scraping the rest of the ice off the car because I knew that the temperatures wouldn't rise enough for the ice to melt.

Wafting across the silent air, I could smell wood burning from Mrs Arling's cottage; it was a smell that made me want to stay at home, cosy up and read a good book, but my appointment was going to change my life forever: so I couldn't miss it. How it was going to change things I didn't know then. If I knew then what I know now, I would have gone back into my cottage and lit a fire. It would have saved many years of heartache and pain.

Teacher's notes

Choose any poem for the pupils to write up as a story. They can embellish it as much as they like but it is good to keep elements the same so it is recognisable. It is a great opportunity to teach settings and characters.

26 Metaphor Poem

Pride is a sunflower hypnotised by the sun.
Calmness is the dark purple deep down in your soul.
Curiosity is a magical world waiting to be discovered.
Wisdom is the mighty mountain that stands and stares at the earth's kingdom.
Deceit is the fire that burns beneath the soil.

Teacher's notes

To create a metaphor you need to use the verb 'is'. You can start with an abstract noun and compare with a plant, country, colour, place, element, animal or planet.

Table 26.1

Abstract noun	is	Comparison (start with a determiner – a/an/the)	Verb (not every line needs a second verb)	Preposition or relative clause	Noun phrase

Pride
Calmness
Curiosity
Wisdom
Deceit
	is	flower
		country
		colour
		place
		animal
		planet
		weather
		season
		insect
		habitat
		transport
			hypnotised
			waiting to be
			    discovered
				by…
				down in…
				beneath…
				which
				who
				that
				where
				whose
					the sun
					your soul
					the earth's
					    kingdoms
					the soil

27 Personification Poem

Fear wandered around the beach touching the hearts of all the men.
Chaos ran riot in the minds of those waiting.
Hope walked the beach confidently inspiring soldiers to want to live.
Anger sizzled through the depths of their hearts.
Memories faded away into the wind.
Dreams died with soldiers taking their last breaths.
Anger lurked forever in the hearts of the brave men.

Teacher's notes

To create the poem:

This is a poem based around Dunkirk. The pupils watched a clip from the film *Atonement* when the soldiers are on the beach. If you do this, be careful to keep the sound down, as there is swearing, and turn the sound up when the music starts.

Choose an abstract noun. Ask what was it doing and where was it doing it? You could then add what it was that it was doing.

First line

Abstract noun – Fear
Doing – wandered
Where – around the beach
Doing what – touching the hearts of all the men. (Noun phrase – 'the hearts of all the men')

Second line

Abstract noun – Chaos
Doing – ran riot
Where – in the minds of those waiting

Third line

Abstract noun – Hope
Doing – walked the beach
How – confidently
Doing what – inspiring soldiers to want to live (Noun phrase – 'soldiers to want to live')

Fourth line

Abstract noun – Anger
Doing – sizzled
Where – through the depths of their hearts (Noun phrase – 'the depths of their hearts')

Fifth line

Abstract noun – Memories
Doing – faded away
Where – into the wind. (Noun phrase – 'the wind')

Sixth line

Abstract noun – Dreams
Doing – died
Where – with soldiers taking their last breaths. (Noun phrase – 'their last breaths')

Seventh line

Abstract noun – Anger
Doing – lurked
Where – in the hearts of the brave men (Noun phrase – 'the hearts of the brave men')

There is a linguistic flexibility in poetry that doesn't quite exist in prose and, used in an enlightened, properly grammatical manner, it can be exploited to great effect in not only broadening a pupil's knowledge, but also in making the process an extremely enjoyable one: that has been the whole object of this chapter.

PART IV

Grammar

28   Nouns and Noun Phrases

Table 28.1

Concrete or common nouns	Everyday tangible objects such as 'table', 'chair' or 'pencil'. They can also be compound nouns such as 'washing machine' and 'football'. Concrete nouns can be count or non-count nouns. You add the suffix '-s' to count nouns while non-count nouns are the same for singular and plural. Count nouns: table/tables, chair/chairs, pencil/pencils Non-count: sheep, deer, coffee, tea, money, water, air, oxygen, rice, salt, butter, luggage, clothing, furniture, basketball, sleeping, junk, weather, homework (same for singular and plural)
Abstract nouns	Emotions: disbelief, love, anxiety, misery, amazement, clarity Characteristics: compassion, courage, determination, beauty, envy Ideas: dream, truth, trust, thought, information Nouns with the following suffixes are often abstract: –tion, –ism, –ity, –ment, –ness, –age, –ance, –ence, –ship, -ability, –acy
Pronouns	See separate sheet
Compound nouns	A compound noun is made up of two or more words, which can either be: Spaced – washing machine Hyphenated – mid-September Closed – bedroom They can be a combination of verbs + noun (washing machine) or adjective + noun (full moon) noun + noun (football), noun + verb (haircut), verb + preposition (check-out), noun + preposition phrase (mother-in-law), preposition + noun (underworld) or a noun + adjective (roomful)
Collective nouns	A count noun that denotes a group of individuals: team, company, majority, assembly, audience, jury, staff, department, faculty, army, council, corporation, family, society, minority, cabinet, school, committee, class and public (not a definitive list) Or a word that tends to describe a group of animals or people. There are some collective nouns that also describe objects, e.g. *an anthology of poems* or *a fleet of cars*. Some nouns can have several collective nouns, e.g. *salmon* can be a *bind of salmon* or a *draught of salmon* or other options are *leap, run, school* and *shoal*.

(continued)

Table 28.1 (*cont.*)

Proper nouns	Names of people or pets: Mary, Tom, Nayla Places: London, Scotland Countries and continents: Asia, Poland Languages: Japanese, Spanish Days of the week/months/festivals: Tuesday, January, Easter Titles of people: Mrs, Lord, Earl, Sir Titles of books: *The Book Thief* The seasons do not have a capital letter: winter, spring, summer, autumn

Noun phrases

1 Often a noun phrase is just a noun or a pronoun:
Dogs love to walk.
She is weary.
It is hot today.

2 Or an article + one or two adjectives + noun:

The sweltering hot sun beat down...
The daunting castle surveyed the king's land.

3 Or a determiner + noun (for an explanation on different types of determiners, see Chapter 29 on pronouns):

Our friends have bought a house in the village.
Those houses are very expensive.
Most children go to school here.
None of the suitcases are mine.

Some words and phrases come after the noun. These are called post-modifiers.

4 Add to + infinitive form of the verb:

You should take *a book to read*.
He could not *buy a long coat to wear*.

5 Add a preposition phrase:

A woman *with a dog*.
The girl *in the car*.
The ship *on the sea*.

In the above examples, the whole phrase is a noun phrase and the underlined words form the preposition phrase. Sometimes two preposition phrases can be added.
That girl over there in a green dress drinking a can of coke.

29 Pronouns

Table 29.1

Personal pronoun		Indefinite pronoun	Reflexive pronoun	Relative pronoun	Possessive pronoun	Possessive adjective
Subject	*Object*	anyone	myself	who	mine	my
		anything	himself	whom	his	her
I	me	anybody	herself	whoever	hers	his
he	him		yourself	whosoever	yours	your
she	her	no one	itself	whomever	its	its
you	you	nobody	oneself	whomsoever	ours	our
it	it	nothing	ourselves	which	theirs	their
we	us		themselves	whichever		
they	them	everybody	yourselves	whose		
		everyone		that		
		everything				
		somebody				
		someone				
		something				

Difference between subject and object personal pronoun

You find the subject personal pronoun at the beginning of a sentence and the object at the end. You cannot start a sentence with an object personal pronoun. For example: 'Me went on holiday'. Likewise, you wouldn't say: 'He went on holiday with I'.

People can confuse when to use 'me' and 'I'. Generally, you find 'I' at the beginning of a sentence and 'me' at the end. When there are two people referred to in a sentence, if you are not sure remove the named person.

> *Mary and I went on holiday* – check for accuracy by removing 'Mary'. *I went on holiday.* (correct)
> *Mary and me went on holiday* – check for accuracy by removing 'Mary'. – *Me went on holiday.* (incorrect)
> *He went on holiday with Mary and I* – check for accuracy by removing 'Mary'. *They went on holiday with I.* (This is not correct; it should be 'me'.)
> *He went on holiday with Mary and me* – check for accuracy by removing 'Mary' – *He went on holiday with me.* (correct)
> *They went on holiday with them.* Not – *Them went on holiday with they.*
> *She went on holiday with him.* Not – *Him went on holiday with she.*

Reflexive pronouns

Reflexive pronouns are used when the subject and the object of the verb refer to the same person or thing:

1 She hurt herself with the hammer.
2 Teachers often blame themselves when they are struggling with the workload.
3 He made himself a cup of tea before watching the film.

Note: The reflexive pronoun is not used with everyday actions such as washing or dressing. We would not say: 'He washed himself this morning'.

The reflexive pronoun can also be used with the addition of 'by', which in the following examples gives the meaning that they are on their own.

1 Why don't they travel by themselves?
2 You could try that by yourself.

Relative pronouns

Table 29.2

Subject	who	which	that
Object	whom	which	that
Possessive	whose	whose	

A relative pronoun is used directly after the person, animal or thing that it is referring to. It adds more detail to the subject. 'Who' and 'whose' is used for people and 'which' is used for things.

Examples of relative pronouns

1 Risotto, <u>which</u> many of us enjoy, is eaten in Italy.
2 This is the film <u>that</u> has been very popular.

3   They met the person <u>whom</u> they wrote to last week.
4   I have a friend <u>whose</u> neighbour has moved to New Zealand.
5   My colleague, <u>who</u> is very good at finding solutions, came up with a logical answer.
6   I remember <u>when</u> we could leave our front doors unlocked.

Difference between possessive pronoun and possessive adjective

A pronoun replaces a noun and an adjective comes before a noun so a possessive pronoun replaces the noun – *It was our house* compared to *It was ours* ('ours' is a possessive pronoun and 'our' is a possessive adjective because it comes before the noun 'house'.)

Other examples:

Table 29.3

Possessive adjective (my, her, his, your, our, their, its) Comes before the noun	Possessive pronoun (mine, his, hers, ours, theirs, its, yours) Replaces the noun
He saw <u>my</u> dog. They are <u>our</u> children. It was <u>their</u> horse.	He saw <u>mine</u>. They are <u>ours</u>. It was <u>theirs</u>.

30 Determiners

Table 30.1

Table 30.1

Article	Demonstrative	Quantifiers		Numbers	Possessive adjective	Other
a an the	this that these those	all any enough less a lot of lots of more most none of some	both each every a few fewer neither either several	one two three four first second third	my your his her its our their	another other

Determiners come before a noun phrase. They can be specific or general, or tell us how many or which order the noun is in or who owns them. They are always found before a noun and are included as part of the noun phrase.

Table 30.2

General determiners	Specific determiners
the my, your, his, her, its, our, their, whose this, that, these, those which	a, an, any, another, other

31 Adjectives

Table 31.1

afraid	compassionate	feisty	hideous
aggressive	dangerous	foolish	hopeful
agile	defiant	fortunate	immediate
agreeable	dependable	frostygloomy	impolite
ajar	difficult	generous	intentjealous
alert	diligent	genuine	jovial
anxious	dim	glum	jubilant
apprehensive	disastrous	fearful	loathsome
bitter	distant	grateful	loyal
blank	dreary	grave	mean
bleak	eager	grim	mindless
breakable	ecstatic	grotesque	miserable
calm	electric	grouchy	motionless
cautious	euphoric	grumpy	powerless
carefree	faint	harmless	reckless
careless	faithful	harmonious	remarkable
clumsy	faraway	harsh	silent
considerate	fast	helpless	unlikeable

Adjectives ending in '–ed' and '–ing'

Table 31.2

abandoned	composed	exhausted	ageing	daring	interesting
aged	concerned	focused	alarming	depressing	irritating
alarmed	crooked	frightened	amazing	disappointing	living
alienated	crowded	good-natured	annoying	dying	horrifying
amazed	curved	horrified	astonishing	embarrassing	humiliating
annoyed	damaged	ill-fated	astounding	enchanting	menacing
astonished	depressed	interested	bewildering	encouraging	puzzling
astounded	deserted	irritated	bewitching	exciting	shocking
bewitched	determined	neglected	boring	exhausting	surprising
bewildered	devoted	puzzled	booming	existing	tempting
big-hearted	disappointed	shocked	captivating	frightening	terrifying
bored	distorted	surprised	charming	glaring	tiring
boomed	embarrassed	tempted	dazzling	gleaming	welcoming
captivated	flustered	terrified	confusing	gripping	worrying
charmed	enchanted	tired	convincing	haunting	
confused	encouraged	welcomed			
convinced	excited	worried			
complicated					

Adjectives describe:

1 Personality – *honest, jealous, selfish*
2 Feelings (both positive and negative) – *excited, lively, energetic, anxious, nervous, vengeful*
3 Appearance – *dirty, dishevelled, glamorous, elegant*
4 Touch – *rough, smooth, gritty*
5 Sound – *screeching, deafening, rhythmical, croaky*
6 Taste – *bitter, sweet, sour, tasteless*
7 Shape – *curved, spherical, flat, deep, crooked*
8 Quantity – *multiple, abundant, empty*
9 Time – *brief, early, ancient*
10 Size – *titanic, enormous, miniscule, tiny*

Comparative and superlative adjectives

Comparative adjectives compare two nouns whereas superlative adjectives compare more than two nouns. For example, *The next door neighbour's house is bigger than mine but the biggest house on the street is on the corner.*
   Adjectives where you just add '–er' or '–est':

1 narrow – narrower – narrowest
2 quick – quicker – quickest
3 tall – taller – tallest
4 shallow – shallower – shallowest
5 hard – harder – hardest
6 calm – calmer – calmest
7 broad – broader – broadest
8 bright – brighter – brightest

Adjectives where you just add '–r' or '–st' (words that end in 'e'):

1 close – closer – closest
2 strange – stranger – strangest
3 polite – politer – politest
4 wide – wider – widest
5 simple – simpler – simplest
6 brave – braver – bravest

Adjectives where you double the last letter and then add '–er' or '–est':

1 big – bigger – biggest
2 thin – thinner – thinnest
3 red – redder – reddest
4 sad – sadder – saddest

Adjectives that end in '–y': change the 'y' to an 'i' and add '–er' or '–est':

1 happy – happier – happiest
2 breezy – breezier – breeziest
3 bumpy – bumpier – bumpiest

4 cloudy – cloudier – cloudiest
5 foggy – foggier – foggiest
6 cosy – cosier – cosiest
7 heavy – heavier – heaviest

Adjectives which don't follow any rule:

1 far – farther – farthest
2 bad – worse – worst
3 good – better – best
4 late – later – latest
5 much – more – most
6 many – more – most
7 little – less – least

Some adjectives do not have the suffix '–er' or '–est' but 'most' or 'more' needs to be added prior to the adjectives:

1 anxious – more anxious – most anxious
2 embarrassed – more embarrassed – most embarrassed
3 nervous – more nervous – most nervous
4 famous – more famous – most famous
5 difficult – more difficult – most difficult

32   Types of Adverbs

Table 32.1

How?	Where?	When?	How often?	How much?	Possibility
angrily	above	afterwards	always	almost	certainly
anxiously	below	again	annually	completely	clearly
cautiously	around	before	constantly	entirely	definitely
courageously	away	early	daily	little	maybe
cruelly	down	lately	hourly	much	obviously
doubtfully	downstairs	never	monthly	too	perhaps
elegantly	everywhere	now	never	totally	possibly
enthusiastically	here	often	occasionally	very	probably
frantically	inside	punctually	often		surely
hungrily	outside	recently	once		
inquisitively	there	soon	regularly		
irritably	up	then	repeatedly		
loudly	upstairs	today	sometimes		
safely	wherever	tomorrow	usually		
shyly		yesterday	yearly		
vivaciously					
well					

Adverbs can sometimes be clumsy, indeed ugly, if overused and applied inexpertly and the use of the verb alone may sometimes be preferable and equally effective.

Adverbs can describe:

1   A verb – *danced recklessly*
2   Another adverb – *too much*
3   An adjective – *too big*

Adverbs can move around a sentence:

1   <u>Quietly</u>, he tiptoed into the cave.
2   He <u>quietly</u> tiptoed into the cave.
3   He tiptoed <u>quietly</u> into the cave.
4   He tiptoed into the cave <u>quietly</u>.

Some adverbs can also be a preposition, such as 'above', 'below', 'after', 'before' and 'about'. It all depends on where the word is in the sentence.

Some adverbs can be both an adjective and an adverb, such as 'down', 'outside' and 'inside'.

33 Subject–Verb Agreement

Present tense and past tense

For subject–verb agreement, add an 's' to the third person singular. For all the other verb tenses the verb is the same.

Table 33.1

Present tense	Past tense
I sing	I sang
He sings	He sang
She sings	She sang
They sing	They sang
We sing	We sung
You sing	You sang
I do	I did
He does	He did
She does	She did
They do	They did
We do	We did
You do	You did

It is the 'to be' verb that confuses pupils the most and needs to be actively taught.

Table 33.2

Past tense	Present tense
I am	I was
He is	He was
She is	She was
They are	They were
We are	We were
You are	You were

The following information is not needed for primary school pupils but is provided for information only. Use a plural verb when two subjects are joined with 'and'.

- Mary and Tom were always arguing.

Subjunctive mood

Normally with the subject 'I, he, she', you use the verb 'was' but when you are using the subjunctive mood you use 'were'.

If I were the queen, I would…
If she were the prime minister, she could…
If he were a fish, he could…

34 Conjunctions

Co-ordinating conjunctions

- and
- but
- nor
- or
- yet
- so
- for

Teachers must be careful with using co-ordinating conjunctions for multi-clause sentences. For it to be a multi-clause sentence, there must be a verb on either side of the conjunction.

With 'and', 'but', or 'nor', whatever word class you find on one side needs to be the same on the other:

Black and white (*adjectives*)
Carefully and slowly (*adverbs*)
Dance and kick (*verbs*)
Pen and pencil (*nouns*)
A black cat and a blue parrot (*noun phrases*)
A cat that dances and a dog that can fly a kite. (*clauses*)
Fearful but determined (*adjectives*)
Quickly but carefully (*adverbs*)
A pen but no pencil (*nouns*)
He was told that he would pass but he would have to work hard. (*clauses*)
Black or white (*adjectives*)
Carefully or quickly (*adverbs*)
Dance or sing (*verbs*)
Pen or pencil (*noun*)
He could either revise for his exam or he could go on holiday. (*clause*)
Neither black nor white (*adjectives*)
Neither carefully nor quickly (*adverbs*)
Neither dancing nor singing (*verbs*)
He is neither playing at the tournament nor going on an adventure holiday. (*clauses*)

To use 'nor', it needs to be preceded with 'neither', 'no', 'never' or 'not'.

When 'for' is being used as a conjunction, it is very difficult to construct a sentence as it is more formal and slightly old-fashioned. It is more commonly used as a preposition.

Conjunction: He was asked to stop for being ridiculously silly.
Preposition: He was given a present for Christmas.

'So' can be used in place of 'because':

1   It snowed heavily so I stayed at home.
2   Because it snowed heavily, I stayed at home.
3   I stayed at home because it snowed heavily.
4   Tim hated his job so he quit.
5   Because Tim hated his job, he quit.
6   Tim quit his job because he hated it.

'So' can act as an adverb:

1   He isn't so bad.
2   The words tumbled out so fast that I could barely understand him.

'Yet' is an alternative to 'but' when we want a stronger effect:

1   Mary can't read music at all yet she is a concert pianist.
2   The sailor's GPS had broken yet he refused to give up on his challenge to cross the Pacific ocean.

'Yet' can also act as an adverb:

1   Yet another cause of trouble…
2   Yet more expense…
3   They may yet succeed…

Subordinating conjunctions

This is not a definitive list of subordinating conjunctions.

Table 34.1

after	even	until
although	even if	when
as	even though	whenever
as long as	if	whereas
as soon as	once	whichever
because	rather than	while
before	since	whilst
despite	unless	

Some subordinating conjunctions act as prepositions such as 'after' and 'before', while others can be adverbs such as 'when', 'after', 'since' and 'before'. It all depends where it is in the sentence and what follows it.

If you start a sentence with a subordinating conjunction, then you need a comma to demarcate the separation with the main clause. For example, *When it rains, it is important to wear a coat.*

35 Verbs

Auxiliary verbs

Table 35.1

Modal verbs	Other
should shall could can will would ought must	do/does/did have/has/had be/am/are/is/was/were

When adding the negative, you need an auxiliary verb. You cannot say 'I walk not to school' but would say 'I do not walk to school'.

The auxiliary verb 'be' is needed to make the continuous and perfect continuous tense. The auxiliary verb 'have' is needed to make the perfect tense and perfect continuous tense. It is combined with the past participle to create the perfect tense.

To ask a question other than using 'where', 'why', 'what', 'when' and 'how', place an auxiliary verb at the front of the sentence.

Present tense

The present tense is used to talk about the present and the future.

Table 35.2

Tense	Examples
Present simple	I walk
Present continuous	I am walking
Present perfect (past participle)	I have seen... or She has seen...
Present perfect continuous	I have been walking She has been walking.

Future tense

How do we denote the future tense?

English has no distinct future tense form of the verb; it is made by preceding the infinitive with 'will' or a modal verb or 'is going' or a time marker.

1 Will – *He will arrive... / I will see you...*
2 Modal verb – *He may arrive... / I could see you...*
3 Is going – *He is going to arrive... / I am going to see...*
4 Time marker – *He arrives tomorrow / I see him every week.*
5 Sometimes it is a combination – *He will arrive tomorrow / He is going to arrive in the afternoon / I could see you in the morning.*

The future tense can also be used when using the subordinating conjunctions 'if', 'when', 'after' and 'until':

1 If it rains tomorrow, we won't go to the park.
2 When I am finished, I will pick him up.
3 After we've had our exam, I will ring you.
4 Until they arrive, we can continue working.

Past tense

The past tense is either made by adding '–ed' ('scared') to regular verbs to create the past tense or the auxiliary verb 'had' + the past participle ('He had seen...'). However, many commonly used verbs are irregular.

The irregular past tense and the past participle are the same:

Table 35.3

Infinitive	Past tense	Past participle
bring	brought	brought
buy	bought	bought
build	built	built
feel	felt	felt
find	found	found
get	got	got
have	had	had
hear	heard	heard
hold	held	held
keep	kept	kept
lead	led	led
leave	left	left
lose	lost	lost
make	made	made
mean	meant	meant
meet	met	met
pay	paid	paid
say	said	said

(continued)

Table 35.3 (*cont.*)

Infinitive	Past tense	Past participle
sell	sold	sold
send	sent	sent
sit	sat	sat
spend	spent	spent
stand	stood	stood
teach	taught	taught
tell	told	told
think	thought	thought
win	won	won

In some case, the infinitive, past tense and past participle are the same:

Table 35.4

Infinitive	Past tense	Past participle
cost	cost	cost
cut	cut	cut
let	let	let
put	put	put
set	set	set

In other cases, all three forms are different:

Table 35.5

Infinitive	Past tense	Past participle
be	was/were	been
begin	began	begun
break	broke	broken
choose	chose	chosen
come	came	come
do	did	done
draw	drew	drawn
drive	drove	driven
eat	ate	eaten
give	gave	given
go	went	gone
know	knew	known
lie	lay	lain
see	saw	seen
speak	spoke	spoken
take	took	taken
wear	wore	worn
write	wrote	written

As with the present tense, the past tense has four different tenses.

Table 35.6

Tense	Example
Past simple	I walked…
Past continuous	I was walking… They were walking…
Past perfect (past participle)	I had spoken… I had seen…
Past perfect continuous	I had been walking.

Subjunctive

For the subjunctive, after certain verbs which express a wish, a command, a suggestion, a desire or a condition that is contrary to fact, use the infinitive form of the verb.

The subjunctive is used after the verbs in the table below, but this is not an exhaustive list:

Table 35.7

to demand (that)	to advise (that)	to recommend (that)
to ask (that)	to suggest (that)	to command (that)
to request (that)	to urge (that)	to insist (that)
to propose (that)	to desire (that)	

Examples:

The teacher asked that Sam work every night. (A request 'asked' followed by the infinitive 'work')

It is suggested that Sam listen more carefully. (A recommendation followed by the infinitive 'listen').

Negative, continuous and passive subjunctive

Negative

The company urged that employees not waste time on Snapchat when at work. (A command 'urged' followed by the infinitive 'waste' plus the negative 'not'.)

I request that you not climb over the fence. (A suggestion followed by the negative then the infinitive verb 'climb'.)

Continuous

It is important that you be waiting at the reception to receive the guests. (A suggestion + to be + continuous/progressive form.)

I propose that we be hiding quietly to surprise him. (A proposition + to be + continuous/progressive form.)

Passive

Sam suggested that Henry be fired instantly. (A suggestion + to be + past simple.)

Should as a subjunctive

The word 'should' can also be used. It tends to be used after the following words: 'insist', 'suggest' and 'recommend'.

Sam recommended that his friend should leave home before it was too late. (A recommendation + should + infinitive form.)

If...were

With the subjunctive mood, you use the verb 'were' rather than 'was'.

We do not say:

I wish she was away.

We do say:

I wish she were away.

36   Inverted Commas

Put inverted commas around the words spoken and start with a capital letter:
   'The programme was really exciting.'
   Add punctuation (.!?,) before the final inverted comma:

1 'You will find him in the lounge.'
2 'What did you think?'
3 'Watch out!'

For clarity, add who said the words. Make sure you add punctuation before closing the inverted comma.
   'I think he's hiding in the cave,' whispered Sam.

Start a new line for each new speaker:
   'I think he's hiding in the cave,' whispered Sam.
   'How do you know?' hissed Ali.

Write who said the words before the inverted commas. A comma is added before you open the inverted commas. Add punctuation before closing the inverted comma.
   Sam whispered, 'I think he's hiding in the cave.'

There could also be a colon before the inverted comma.
   Mr Jones, an eyewitness, said: 'The car just kept on rolling.'

When you divide a sentence by who said it, you don't use a capital letter after the second inverted comma if the sentence continues.
   'If you think you can leave your litter here,' she said sternly, 'you had better think again!'

When you divide two sentences to show who is speaking, both opening inverted commas need to be followed by a capital letter.
   'You won't be able to find him,' she noted. 'You will have to come back tomorrow.'

To avoid stories being lost in speech, restrict the pupils to a maximum of three sentences in this format. As the pupils become more comfortable with the grammar, encourage them to mix the style of inverted commas. There are four sentences here to demonstrate a mix of the types of usage.
   Sam whispered, 'I think he's hiding in the cave.'
   'I know,' hissed Ali.
   'You always seem to know everything,' Sam said, raising his eyes heavenward. 'Do you know how irritating that is?'
   'Let's hide behind the tree,' Ali suggested, 'so we can catch him when he leaves.'

37 How to Use Colons and Semi-colons

The colon

The colon is a powerful punctuation mark, the second strongest in the language between a semi-colon and a full stop. It is subtle in its application, immensely valuable in conveying the writer's intention by extending the application of the original statement.

It is used:

1 To introduce something. The wording before the colon makes a statement and the words after the colon expand and enhance the meaning of the opening words. Its most commonly quoted use in this context is the production of a list.

    a The list can be simple – *Gavin took all his equipment to school: his books, his trainers, his mobile and his soccer boots.*

    b The list can be much more complex than this, extending the simple nouns by the addition of adjectives and qualifying clauses – *Gavin was feeling terrible: he had a headache which was making his vision blurred, he had butterflies in his stomach because of the impending morning test and he was frightened because he hadn't done his homework.*

    c The list can take the form of an instruction – *Contact us by e-mail: jack@gmail.com.*

    d Other than a list it can be used with a simple statement incorporating a short introduction followed by an explanatory statement – *Football: a boy's dream pastime and a grown man's sole interest.*

2 To extend, enhance, emphasise, elaborate upon or explain the words grouped before or after the colon itself, e.g. *Her day started at dawn and was never finished until she went to bed: collecting water, baking bread, lighting fires, cleaning, washing, helping in the fields, mending clothes and so on.*

3 To introduce bullet points, e.g. *I think we ought to say:*

    a *go home*

    b *mend your ways*

    c *return to duty*

4 To insert before quotations, e.g. *Winston Churchill said: 'Never before in the...'* This is now going out of fashion.

5 To make an impact in a short, incisive way, particularly in modern journalism, e.g. [Talking about an aged and difficult film star] *She still doesn't indulge in charm but what she does have is something more precious: grace.* Here, the short, incisive part of the sentence on one side of the colon can be either at the beginning or end of the sentence.

The semi-colon

Semi-colons, in simple terms, are used to divide up more complicated sentences and separate the different parts, representing a longer pause than a comma:

1   They are used to separate main clauses and mark the boundaries between independent clauses: e.g.
    It was very early; everybody was still in bed, asleep.
2   They are also used when listing nouns that have expanded descriptions.
    I will buy rye bread from Germany; fresh organic goat's milk from the Alps; delicious homemade straw-
    berry and rhubarb jam; and Jersey cream from the supermarket.
3   Sometimes if a sentence is closely connected in form and meaning to the previous one and suggests
    that only a light break rather than a heavy one (a full stop) is needed, it is better to use a semi-colon:
    e.g. *I thought you were wrong; thinking about it more carefully, you may be right.*
4   They are often placed just before particular words like *however, therefore, as a result, consequently* in
    a transitional phrase. There is always a comma after a transitional phrase, e.g. *The paper is stuck in my*
    printer; consequently, I can't print this note out for checking.

Be careful not to overdo the use of the semi-colon; if you do, you'll annoy your readers. It is a tool to
expand sentences when there is an overuse of short sentences and a need to vary the length of sentences
is needed.

38   Passive and Active Sentences

Transitive verbs (verbs that have a noun phrase as an object) have both an active and passive form.

Table 38.1

Active	Passive
The mouse scared the elephant.	The elephant was scared by the mouse.
The boys have smashed the window.	The window has been smashed by the boys.
The cats chased the dog.	The dog was chased by the cats.

For each passive sentence you could omit who it was 'by'. This can keep the subject hidden.

1   The elephant was scared. (by the mouse)
2   The window has been broken. (by the boys)
3   The dog was chased. (by the cats)

The passive form is made up of the verb – 'be' – with a past participle.

Table 38.2

Be – past participle				
Megan/I/people	is/am/are	given	presents at Christmas	by family and friends.
She/they	was/were	taken	to the doctors	by her mother.
The company	have/has/had been	bought out		by a larger company.
A drink/drinks	was/were being	served		by experienced staff.
The story	will be	finished		by the children.
We/she	might have/has/had been	asked	to dance	by the organisers.

The verb 'get' can be used in the passive form:

'She might get given a certificate.'

The verb 'to get' is quite clumsy; usually there are other verbs which could be used instead.

A good indicator of whether a sentence is active or passive is whether you can add 'by' to the end of the sentence.

She might get given a certificate by her teacher.

Some verbs, frequently used in the passive form, are followed by the infinitive form of the verb preceded by 'to'.

Mary has been allowed <u>to dance</u> in the show. (by the director)
The meeting is scheduled <u>to end</u> at one. (by the chairperson)
The children have been told <u>to be quiet</u> several times. (by the teacher)